Praise for Lauren Slater's
Prozac Diary

"A gentle, illuminating memoir."
—*The New York Times Book Review*

"Thoughtful, lucid." —*The New Yorker*

"The 'chemistry' of *Prozac Diary* is 'beautiful.'"
—*The New York Times*

"Tightly bound by its humor and intelligence . . . Slater's writing is confessional without being sentimental, honest without being overbearing." —*The Boston Globe*

"Witnessing Slater's glorious power with words is as evocative and moving as hearing first words. Making the transition to wellness with Slater is a small dose of miracle for her lucky readers." —*Newsday*

"An enormously poetic and ebullient writer—and certainly Prozac's most honest narrator yet—Slater is still grappling with 'the difficulty and compromise of cure' when she has to take a pill in order to join the world."
—*Elle*

"Rich and provocative." —*The Boston Phoenix*

"Other writers have documented the sensation of chemical self-annihilation, but none have achieved Slater's in-the-trenches immediacy or eloquence." —*Mirabella*

"Slater reminds us that a writer's true gift—and power—lies in the ability to generously turn what seems like a specific experience into a universal one. While nominally about Slater's struggle with mental illness, this poetically told tale becomes not merely about Prozac and the author's journey to health, but the journey to finding oneself."   —*Entertainment Weekly*

"Slater wonders whether the drug will make her a worse writer. About that she needn't have worried."
                              —*The Philadelphia Inquirer*

"Slater details her journey to wellness in a colorful and candid manner that evokes both sorrow for the many years she struggled through mental illness and tentative hope for her future."
                              —*Rocky Mountain News*

"[Lauren Slater's] voice flows clearly and yet dreamily, as if she's just a bit detached from the story, and always with a rare kind of elegant honesty."   —*The Hartford Courant*

"Slater writes, in fresh, descriptive language, how health can be oddly disorienting to a person whose identity has been built, brick by sharp brick, out of illness."
                              —*The Oregonian*

"Slater is frank, engaging and closely descriptive. Her worry that long-term use has diminished her creativity should be allayed by this luminous, cautiously optimistic memoir."
                              —*Publishers Weekly*

"In this both tragic and comedic tale, Slater is forthright and fresh about her journey to wholeness. Although the jury is still out on whether Prozac is actually beneficial, her honesty will touch even the hardest soul." —*Booklist*

"Heartfelt but never mawkish; eloquent but never slick; a lyrical account of a drug that has caused mounds of controversy."
                              —*Kirkus Reviews*

PENGUIN BOOKS

PROZAC DIARY

Lauren Slater is the author of the acclaimed *Welcome to My Country*. She has a master's degree in psychology from Harvard University and a doctorate from Boston University. Her work was chosen for The Best American Essays of 1994 and 1997. She is the winner of the 1993 New Letters Literary Award in creative nonfiction and of the 1994 Missouri Review Award. She was also a nominee for the 1998 National Magazine Award.

LAUREN SLATER

Prozac Diary

PENGUIN BOOKS

PENGUIN BOOKS

Published by the Penguin Group

Penguin Putnam Inc., 375 Hudson Street,
New York, New York 10014, U.S.A.
Penguin Books Ltd, 27 Wrights Lane, London W8 5TZ, England
Penguin Books Australia Ltd, Ringwood, Victoria, Australia
Penguin Books Canada Ltd, 10 Alcorn Avenue,
Toronto, Ontario, Canada M4V 3B2
Penguin Books (N.Z.) Ltd, 182–190 Wairau Road,
Auckland 10, New Zealand

Penguin Books Ltd, Registered Offices:
Harmondsworth, Middlesex, England

First published in the United States of America by Random House, Inc., 1998
Reprinted by arrangement with Random House, Inc.
Published in Penguin Books 1999

10 9 8 7 6 5 4 3 2 1

Grateful acknowledgment is made to PolyGram Music Publishing for permission to reprint four lines from "I Will Survive" by Frederick J. Perren and Dino Fekaris. Copyright © 1978 by PolyGram International Publishing, Inc. and Perren-Vibes Music, Inc. All rights reserved. Used by permission.

THE LIBRARY OF CONGRESS HAS CATALOGUED
THE HARDCOVER EDITION AS FOLLOWS:
Slater, Laura.
Prozac Diary/Lauren Slater.
p.   cm
ISBN 0-679-45721-6 (hc.)
ISBN 0 14 02.6394 2 (pbk.)
1. Slater, Lauren.   2. Mentally ill—United States—Biography.
3. Fluoxetine.   4. Mental illness—Chemotherapy—Case studies.
I. Title.
RC464.S58A3   1998   616.89'0092—dc21
[B]   97–35727

Printed in the United States of America
Set in Perpetua
Designed by J.K. Lambert

FOR YOU, BEN.

With the exception of Dr. Bruce Alexander, the names of the characters in this memoir have been changed, as have some details about them and the events recounted here.

ACKNOWLEDGMENTS

Karen Propp read every version of this manuscript, and I don't think I could have completed it without her kindness and intelligence. Nadine Boughton and Pagan Kennedy were keen critics and great company on Thursday nights. Lisa Schiffman listened to drafts long-distance; David Fore, Jennifer Coon, Lisa Tucker, Tracy Slater, Audrey Schulman, and Molly Froelich's comments were helpful throughout. AfterCare Services, my place of employment, granted me the scheduling flexibility to be able to work on this book. As usual, Elizabeth Graver's ongoing support is part of the foundation on which much of my writing rests.

I am grateful to have as my agent Kimberly Witherspoon, and her associates Maria Massie, Josh Greenhut, and Gideon Weil. I am also grateful, and lucky, to have as my editor Kate Medina, to whom I owe much thanks.

To get there, you turn left off the highway and drive down the road bordered on one side by pasture. And then, a radio song or so later, you turn right into the hospital's gated entrance, easing your car up the slope that leads to the turreted place where he waits. Safety screens cover all the windows. The stairs are steep, and exit signs cast carmine shadows on the concrete floors. Four flights you must travel, and then down several serpentine corridors, before you finally come to his office.

I had never been here before. I had never heard the word *Prozac* before. It was 1988, the drug just released. I was to be one of the first to take Prozac, and, even though I didn't know this then, one of the first to stay on it for the next ten years, experiencing what long-term existence on this new medication is actually like.

The Prozac Doctor is a busy man. He sees thirty, forty, sometimes fifty patients a day. He is handsome in ways you don't expect your medicine man to be. He has shining black hair and beautiful loafers made of leather so fresh you can practically see the hide still ripple with life. He wears one simple gold band on a finger as tapered as a pianist's, topped with a chip of nacreous nail sanded to perfect smoothness. He is host as well as doctor, and that first time, as well as every time thereafter, he invites me in, standing behind his desk and ushering me forward with stately sweeps of his hand, bowing ever so slightly in a room where you half expect caterers carrying platters of shrimp to emerge from the shadows.

"Sit, Ms. Slater," he said to me the morning we met. He gestured to a deep seat, and I sat. There was a silence between us then, a kind of weighted silence, a grand silence, like the sort you hear before a symphony begins.

And that day was the beginning, the bare beginnings of a story very little like the popular Prozac myths— a wonder drug here, a drug that triggers violence there. No. For me the story of Prozac lies not between these poles but entirely outside of them, in a place my doctor was not taught to get to—the difficulty and compromise of cure, the grief and light of illness passing, the fear as the walls of the hospital wash away and you have before you this—this strange planet, pressing in.

—

But that first day, there was just Prozac pressing in. I looked around me at the office. On the doctor's desk I saw a Lucite clock with the word PROZAC embossed across the top. I saw a marble mount holding four pens with PROZAC etched down their flanks. The pads of paper resting on his bookshelf were the precise size and shape of hors d'oeuvre napkins, and all had PROZAC in fancy script across their borders, like the name of some new country club.

"What is this stuff?" I asked. I heard my voice repeat itself in my ears, as so many sounds seemed to do lately, the screech of brakes, birdsong nipping at my brain.

The doctor leaned back in his seat. "Prozac," he said, "is the chemical compound fluoxetine hydrochloride." He told me it had a three-ring chemical structure similar to that of other medications I'd tried in the past but that its action on the body's serotonin system made it a finer drug. He told me about the brain chemical serotonin and its role in OCD—obsessive-compulsive disorder—the most recent of my many ills, for me the nattering need to touch, count, check, and tap, over and over again. He told me about synapses and clefts, and despite the time he took with me that day, I felt him coming at me across a gulf.

He had all the right gestures. His knowledge was impeccable. He made eye contact with the subject, meaning me. But still, there was something about the way the Prozac Doctor looked at me, and the very technical way he spoke to me, that made me feel he was viewing me generally—swf, long psych history, five hospitalizations for depression and anxiety-related problems, poor medication response in past, now referred as outpatient for sudden emergence of OCD—as opposed to me, viewing me, in my specific skin.

My skin: had little white lines on it from where I used to cut. It had always crisped easily in the summer sun.

My ears: knew the difference between real and imaginary sounds. That said, they sometimes heard voices, which doctors in the hospitals had told me was a sign not of psychosis but of dissociation. There was a blue baby who cried in my ears. There was a girl in a glass case, who talked to me. The world was full of many sounds—rushings, whirrings, soft and thunderous—and this was both a pleasure and a problem.

My hands: had become a problem. Once they had

been conduits for pleasure. When I was a child they had held leaves and rabbits. Today, however, they were one of the reasons I was here. They were the part of me that seemed to have the OCD, tense and seeking, tapping things forty, fifty, sixty times. Not people, thank God, but objects, like stove switches, gas dials. Sometimes I looked at my hands and remembered them as they used to be, fine-boned, indigo-veined, lined with the tracery of all they had touched. Not now, though. From my hands I had learned grief. I had learned how the body can leave you, before you have left it.

—

I wanted to tell the Prozac Doctor about my hands. I wanted to splay them across his desk and say, "Look at them. What are they seeking?" I wanted him to touch my hands, not really an odd desire, the laying on of hands a practice as ancient as the Bible itself. The Prozac Doctor was biblical to me. I invited him to take on that role, the role every sick person needs her healer to play—not only technician, but poet, priest, theologian, and friend. I know this was asking a lot, poor man, but few people are as full of need and desire as the patient.

Instead, he reached down, opened a desk drawer, and pulled out a sample pill packet. He did not need to ask me many questions, as he had my entire chart before him, thick as an urban phone book. The packet was rather unimpressive, plain white, with a perforated top. To my surprise, he lifted it to his lips and tore at it with his teeth, then gently tapped at it until a smooth pill slid from its foiled pouch into the clean cup of his palm.

There it lay, cream and green. Tiny black letters were stamped down its side—DISTA—which sounded to me like an astronomy term, the name of a planet in another galaxy. On and on my mind went, making from this small capsule many private metaphors—it was candy, no poison; protein, no plastic.

I wanted to say these things to the Prozac Doctor. But he held himself so politely, angled away from contact. And, after all, he was a busy man, pressured by insurance companies to see throngs of patients, all with their own little paint box of multiple metaphors. Where would he have found the time to explore with me the private poem of the medicine that would soon be mine, a poem that had, as its first stanza, some song about failure? Having tried for the past three years to achieve stability on my own, determined to do it, I was here again, sick with this OCD. How could that be? I was incomplete, apparently, without the pill that was, among other things, a plug to stopper some hole in my soul. Perhaps the hole came from a neuronal glitch, the chemical equivalent of a dropped stitch in the knitted yarn of my brain. Or maybe the hole was between my mother and me. Because when I looked at the pill I also saw her, the little capsule of her sports car we would speed in, clean and compact, screeching to a halt in front of the florist's, where she bought armloads of orchids. And then to the butcher's, where she purchased great red wheels of beef. Nothing was ever enough, for there was no plug to stopper the hole in her soul, no pill.

My pill. Sitting, still, in the Prozac Doctor's palm but moving me backward in time, forward into hope. Much has been said about the meanings we make of illness, but what about the meanings we make out of cure? Cure is complex, disorienting, a revisioning of the self, either subtle or stark. Cure is the new, strange planet, pressing in. The doctor could not have known. And that made me, as it does every patient, only more alone.

—

"We will start," he said to me, "with twenty milligrams a day, a single capsule, although OCD, unlike depression, usually requires a higher dose." He showed me how, if the dose made me nauseous, I could split the pill and try half, and when I asked him what, exactly, was inside, he told me the story of the drug's design. He told me about Eli Lilly's campus in Indiana, where Prozac was first made, how a man raised rats and then ground their brains into something called a synaptosome, which became this medicine. He told me how Prozac marked a revolution in psychopharmacology because of its selectivity on the serotonin system; it was a drug with the precision of a Scud missile, launched miles away from its target only to land, with a proud flare, right on the enemy's roof.

I pictured the proud flare. I pictured the grounds of Eli Lilly, green and winding. Inside, the labs were clean. White-coated technicians were plucking the gray matter from rats, extracting the liquid transmitters, some kind of healing wet.

I hoped then.

I hoped to be helped.

—

And yet, I did not take this new pill. Back at home, in the basement apartment where I lived, I looked and looked at it. I touched it to the tip of my tongue, then moved it away. This was not a tease, the drawn-out flirtation that will later come to love. This was fear. Maybe more than anything else, taking a pill, especially a recently developed psychotropic pill about which researchers have more questions than answers, is always an exercise in the existential, because whatever happens happens to your body alone. Each time you swallow a pill you are swallowing not only a chemical compound but yourself unmoored; you are swallowing the sea, the drift and the drown. A pill makes the inscrutable Sartre solid, brings to life the haunting solitude of a Munch painting. It is not the doctor's job to populate the painting, but if he has a flair for the medical arts, maybe he will. The Prozac Doctor, for all his style, couldn't. Psychopharmacology is the one branch of medicine where there is no need for intimacy; neither knives nor stories are an essential part of its practice. And in its understandable glee that it might finally move psychiatry into a position as respectable as surgery, it risks forgetting, or maybe never learning, what even many a surgeon knows: that you must smooth the skin, that you must stop by the bedside in your blue scrub suit, that language is the kiss of life.

I had a dream one night about the Prozac Doctor. This was four or five days after our first visit in what would become over a decade-long relationship. I dreamt I saw him in the supermarket and he was buying bread. He was in a dark suit with brass buttons, and he approached several loaves, newly baked, lying on wooden boards, each with a scar down its center. I knew the Prozac Doctor was hungry, because I could feel his pangs in me. I could feel how he wanted to crack the caul of his professional persona. I thought I should help him, that because I was a patient and knew about proneness and heat, I could, maybe, instruct. Perhaps this is the patient's task. Perhaps in every good medical encounter each party must try to save the other.

So I showed the Prozac Doctor the bread. I showed him how to test it for firmness, how to split it down its scar and spread the salve of butter on it. He lifted a loaf—honey-wheat, I think—and from the hidden folds of his jacket pocket took out a stethoscope. I nodded at him, and he pressed the stethoscope against the breast of the bread, eyes half closed, listening, listening, and then the bread breathed back—a rush and a whir—sounds both thunderous and soft in my ears. I woke up.

And later on that day I got up the courage to take my first dose. A dream doctor, apparently, can bear witness and hold out the promise of tenderness almost as well as a real doctor. It is very fashionable in medical science these days to talk about the power of visualization in healing. Your cancer cells are turning fresh as healthy heartland apples; your tumor is bearing milk. Although I say this tongue in cheek, I am serious too. Perhaps we should instruct patients, especially psychiatric patients, to visualize not only the transformation of their illness but the transformation of their doctors as well. Maybe out of such visualizations—insistent, intense, articulated—we will help to midwife our medicine men.

I held the pill in my hand and then washed it down with water. Afterward, things seemed so quiet. My eyes and ears were tilted inward, listening, looking. I felt what might have been a burning in my chest, something scampering up around my heart. Side effect? Serious? A start? It was too early to know. So I sat on a stool in my kitchen, and I conjured up the Prozac Doctor with his hand on a curve of crusty bread, the hide of fresh whole wheat. I stroked my own arm. I tried for calmness. I thought of yeast and how it works, bubbles of fermentation, little spheres of oxygen that must be kneaded, how maybe every good rising is a combination of chemicals and touch.

EVALUATION AND TREATMENT PLAN

Patient Name: Lauren J. Slater
Patient Age: 26
Evaluating Physician: Dr. Morris Koskava
Date of Evaluation: May 22, 1988

1. Presenting Problem and History:

Patient currently presents with symptoms that meet the criteria for Obsessive-Compulsive Disorder. However this diagnosis can be seen as secondary as opposed to primary. Patient reports OCD, with its attendant compulsions to count, check, and wash, emerged rather suddenly and unexpectedly w/in last few months. However, patient does have a long history of psychopathology prior to the manifestation of her present complaint. Has in the past attempted suicide, and engaged in self-mutilating behaviors, including anorexia, that resulted in psychiatric hospitalizations: dates, 1977, 1979, 1983, 1984, 1985. Record indicates patient has carried a diagnosis of Borderline Personality Disorder since 19 years of age, and a diagnosis of major depression, severe and recurrent, beginning in her early—

How do you describe emptiness? Is it the air inside a bubble, the darkness in a pocket, snow? I think, yes, I was six or seven when I first felt it, the dwindling that is depression. I was sitting on the porch, and it was summer, the air jammed with heat. From inside the house I could hear my mother, hear her heels tapping against the gleaming wood of our foyer floor, and I could imagine her legs, lean as a thoroughbred's and glistening beneath their net of nylons. She always wore nylons, summer or winter, and her hair was a compilation of chemical color that started as blond and then moved into brass, sometimes frosted, sometimes dark.

I couldn't reach her. I was never able to reach her. Maybe she moved at a pace too fast. Maybe she was too sad. She held herself stiff, a lacquered lady. I think because I couldn't feel her, I couldn't feel myself. I pictured my body's organs to look like pieces of jewelry. My heart was a brooch, my stomach a diamond. Open me up, please. Inside I am sawdust and silk.

When I was six, seven, eight, I liked to go to the candy store in the center of our small suburban town. I could walk there, and I had pennies. The store was called Barbar Jean's, and Barbar Jean himself worked the counter and cash register. He was a good man; of that I am sure. Entering his dark store from the blazing heat of a New England summer, you met first with total obscurity, which slowly lifted to show shelves holding every imaginable sweetness, curved plastic jars stuffed with fireballs, strings of black licorice swinging from hooks, soft drinks floating in a wooden barrel. I moved around the store, each time observing its bounty—food to fill me—and I sampled everything except the chocolate babies. Heaped in a glass globe, they were tiny things, bite-sized babies, with minuscule hands etched from fudge, faces with slitted eyes and pinprick mouths, strands of hair sketched in their Negroid skulls. They scared me. I was drawn to them, and I would always pause to peer at them— larvae, covey—the glass jar permanently pregnant with quiet.

"And what would the Chief like today?" Barbar Jean always asked. Take note—he called me Chief. He might have called me Chief because he knew I was a rich girl, but I think not. Even back then, at the very beginning, I carried myself with a kind of confidence and verve, and I have yet to understand how energy can so easily coexist with what is hollow.

A fireball. Or malted milk. Maybe a chewy fish or, if it was very hot, a Coke. I didn't feast in his store but rather brought my bounty home and ate it in my bedroom, in secret.

People want to know about the big things. Did she pierce you, did the dishes crash down? But these are not the events memory always makes as its markers. We never got along. What I most vividly recall is the summer day I saw her ironing my clothes. Why, when we had three housekeepers and a butler to boot, she was ironing my clothes, I do not know. But there she was, in the laundry room, with its washer and dryer and boxes of Tide. The iron sat up on its heel, hissing. The heat turned tactile as steam rose. She picked up a pair of my pants from the laundry basket, pants I'd played hard in, pants I was Chief in, pants with ripped seams and holes in the knees, and then she went to work on them. She lowered the hot block down and moved with fast, angry strokes, pressing with her weight, flattening and cauterizing all at once, and I felt, for the first time, not only how intensely but how erotically she wanted to erase me. I shivered. The iron was on my thighs, moving up the silver zipper of my crotch.

Later on that day, at Barbar Jean's, I bought my first and only chocolate baby. "Just one?" Barbar Jean said.

"One," I said.

One he gave me.

I took it outside, into the streets of the town. I looked at my goody. I didn't chew into the chocolate baby. I placed it very carefully on the pad of my tongue. I felt it move down my throat and into my stomach, and when it mixed, at last, with my blood, the baby turned blue. This I take as a truth. I also take as a truth that at night, while from the floor below me my mother paced, I could hear the baby turn and sometimes cry. I could talk to it, and it could talk to me. Later on, I would populate my innards with more figurative people, but this was the first. It was not, understand, a bad thing. I was not crazy. Even back then I could sense how the language of emptiness, the language of loss, evaded me. Now my emptiness had weight and presence. I had moved into metaphor, a significant developmental step. Perhaps even a cause for celebration. I called the presence Blue Baby. Its deadness, in its own way, was alive. This was my first love. This was my world.

When I was a girl I loved fevers and flus and the muzzy feeling of a head cold, all these states carrying with them the special accouterments of illness, the thermometer with its lovely line of red mercury, the coolness of ice chips pressed to a sweaty forehead, and best of all, a distant mother coming to your bedside with tea. In illness the world went wonderfully warped, high temperatures turning your pillow to a dune of snow and bringing the night sky, with its daisy-sized stars, so close to your bed you could touch it, and taste the moon.

I loved my illnesses. I loved my regal mother bending to the mandates of biology, allowing me to rest and watch TV. She even read me stories, sitting at my bedside. In the dim room, her wedding ring twinkled like the eye of an elf, and her hands brushed stray strands of hair from my face.

Illness was a temporary respite, a release from the demands of an alienating world. In my world, women had hair as hard as crash helmets. In my world, girls did not play. They practiced: the piano, the flute, French, manners so refined they made all speech stiff. Illness was not stiff. You went kaput. Fluids rushed in and rushed out, your nose got gummy, and frogs hopped around in your chest. Getting better was a grief. One morning you woke up and your fever had fled. Your throat felt depressingly fine. You looked across your orange carpet and saw your black patent dancing shoes, your child-sized golf clubs. You saw your French and Hebrew workbooks, with all those verbs you would have to conjugate before dinner tonight. You wanted to weep.

Prozac, too, made me want to weep. Prozac, too, was a grief, because it returned me to the regular world with consequences I never expected. The first few days on the medication I vomited a lot, and I got headaches. The Prozac Doctor, Koskava, told me these were normal side effects in the early stages.

At first I didn't think much of the stuff. I was as obsessive as ever, needing to touch, tap, knock, and count my way through the day. I did notice I was sleeping a little better, although my dreams were jagged and relentless, filled with images of tide pools and the sounds of shouts.

And then one morning, about five days after I'd first started the drug, I opened my eyes at eight A.M. I'd turned out my light at midnight, which meant I'd gotten, for the first time in many months, a seamless eight hours of sleep. It was a Saturday, and stripes of sun were on my walls. I sat up.

Something was different. I looked at my hand. It was the same hand. I touched my face—nose, cheeks, chin, all there. I rubbed my eyes and went into the kitchen.

The kitchen, too, was the same—table, two pine chairs, gray linoleum buckled and cracked along the floor. The sink still dripped. The grass moved against my window ledge. All the same, all different. What was it?

A piano tuner used to come to our house when I was young. He was a blind man, his eyes burnt-out holes in his head, his body all bent. I remember how strange he looked against the grandeur of our lives, how he stooped over that massive multitoothed instrument and tweaked its tones. The piano never looked any different after he'd worked on it, but when I pressed a C key or the black bar of an F minor, the note sprung out richer, as though chocolate and spices had been added to a flat sound.

This was what was different. It was as though I'd been visited by a blind piano tuner who had crept into my apartment at night, who had tweaked the ivory bones of my body, the taut strings in my skull, and now, when I pressed on myself, the same notes but with a mellower, fuller sound sprang out.

This is what was different—tempo, tone. Not sight, for everything looked the same. Not smell, for everything smelled the same. Not pitch, for the vibrations of the world were just as they'd always been. To describe the subtle but potent shift caused by Prozac is to tussle with failing words, sensations that seep beyond language. But that doesn't make it any less miraculous. Doctors assure the public that psychotropic drugs don't get a patient high; rather, supposedly, they return the patient to a normal state of functioning. But what happens if such a patient, say, myself, for instance, has rarely if ever experienced a normal state of functioning? What happens if such a patient has spent much of her life in mental hospitals, both pursuing and pursued by one illness after another? What happens if "regular life" to such a person has always meant cutting one's arms, or gagging? If this is the case, then the "normal state" that Prozac ushers in is an experience in the surreal, Dalí's dripping clock, a disorientation so deep and sweet you spin. Thus Prozac, make no mistake about it, blissed me out and freaked me out and later on, when the full force of health hit me, sometimes stunned me with grief.

—

I want to describe it. I'm sorry, for there is nothing that bores me quite so much as people who regale me with tales of their acid trips, how the walls breathed and the unity in the world became palpably apparent. Still, descriptions of acid trips, relentless as they may sometimes be, are a staple of sixties literature, characterizing the mood of an entire generation. My generation, of course, is the Prozac generation, and no generation can be complete without a record of the substances that have irrevocably altered it.

So don't let anyone tell you different. If you have been sick for a long, long time, Prozac may make you high. It probably won't make you high the way pot and acid do; it will make you high by returning you to a world you've forgotten or never quite managed to be a part of, but a world, nevertheless, that you at first fit into with the precision of a key to a lock or a neurotransmitter to its receptor.

For me, as I've said, it was a question of tempo and tone. Everything seemed to be moving according to a different rhythm, 4/4 now 2/2, a smoothing out or slowing down. It was, to date, the single most stunning experience of my life, although later it would unfold with ever more complexity, even danger. But at that moment, standing in my kitchen on an early Saturday morning, I soaked in it. A cat loped by. Clouds meandered in the sky. But best, absolutely best of all, were the surfaces. They no longer compelled me—to touch, knock, tap, the relentless obsessive itch that had almost put me back in the hospital. I walked around my apartment, curious. Yes, a streak of grease on the window. Yes, the prongs of a plug. I noticed it all and didn't seem to care. Somehow, my attention had become flexible, swiveling left, now right, with such ease it made me giddy.

I remember running my hands over a lot of things to test the medicine's power. I remember standing at my sink and fiddling with the faucets, turning them on and then off, but not completely, so the washers still dripped. It was OK. There would be no punishing flood. God was good. I turned the stove on, watched the blue ring of fire flare at the base of the burner, watched it recede as I swiveled the dial down, down, heat sucked back into blackness. Without checking, I trusted what I saw; the stove was off. God was good. Picking up my transistor radio, I gauged its little ridged dials. I heard bells and violins, settled back on my bed to listen to what I thought might be Bach. In my blissed-out state it took me many moments to realize that what was entering my mind was not Bach but Muzak.

—

I dozed off to the Muzak, and when I woke up again it was nearing noon. The sun, slanting through my basement-apartment windows, had an odd and quiet quality; its rays seemed to rustle, like a silk dress.

Not sure what to do next, I considered lunch. I pulled my menus out from the night-table drawer, the menus I, a person of boot-camp rigidity, had for the past several years carefully calculated for their calories, proteins, and fats. The day's menu suggested tuna, a single scoop with low-cal mayonnaise, two unsalted rice cakes, and seltzer water. I'd been eating this meal, or meals just like it, for a long time. I couldn't quite believe that. Low-cal mayonnaise? Rice cakes? I wanted something richer, something whipped and frozen.

Maybe I should skip lunch and go right to my afternoon workout. But I felt too calm for the rigors of a run. Well, then, what could I do? What could I do? An odd sort of sadness came over me then. I supposed I could read, fifty pages a day, the requirement I'd always set for myself.

I went over to my bookshelves, makeshift boards on bricks. I had a lot of books, most of them nonfiction, because I'd always felt that in nonfiction, specifically in the disciplines of psychology, philosophy, and theology, I might find clues about ways to live my life. I scanned the spines, saw titles like *Fear and Trembling* and *Man's Search for Meaning*. I had loved these sorts of books, loved untangling the dense mats of seaweed-like sentences, underlining and starring meaningful passages that I took in as a kind of elite self-help, which is probably what all this stuff really amounts to anyway. But now, well, now I stood by my bookshelves a little lost. They were full of death and anxiety, the spines seeming to exude cold clouds. I had no desire to read Kierkegaard. Maybe something a little lighter, like Viktor Frankl. I picked up *Man's Search for Meaning* and skimmed through the thumbed pages. I read my many beloved Frankl sentences, such as, "A man who for years had thought he had reached the absolute limit of all possible suffering now found that suffering has no limits, and that he could suffer still more, and more intensely still." I spent a long time staring at that sentence. Over and over in my life it had brought me comfort, for Frankl, along with other existentialists, is devoted to the meaning and dignity of pain. I had lived my life by these kinds of banners, only now, searching the sentence, I found little in it that really resonated deep in my bones. I had a cerebral sort of appreciation for the sentence, or, perhaps, an appreciation based in memory, the way one remembers with fondness a past partner whom one no longer loves.

I slipped the book back among its companions. *Whom one no longer loves.* Herein lay the problem. A new kind of anxiety started to sprout in me, a duller, more distant anxiety, the first glimmers of what would later come to grief. For the world as I had known it my whole life did not seem to exist. Not only had Prozac—thank all the good gods in the world—removed the disabling obsessive symptoms; it seemed, as well, to have tweaked the deeper proclivities of my personality. Who was I? Where was I? Everything seemed less relevant—my sacred menus, my gustatory habits, the narratives that had had so much meaning for me. Diminished. And in their place? Ice cream.

I went outside to get it. The ice cream truck had chugged up my street, paused by the curb, playing its carnival tunes. A Saturday in deep spring, children swarmed, sweaty money in their little fists. I joined them, the only adult in sight. I felt foolish, my breasts too big, stubble of dark hair on my legs. Now I think I made an apt choice to join the children, for I was a child myself in some significant ways, unschooled in the

habits of health. I scanned the menu board—rocket
cones, Malibu bars, grape pops. When it was my turn, I
ordered something called an orange freeze. I sat on the
front stoop of my apartment building to eat it, tearing
the paper off, holding the wooden stick, biting down on
the bar's bright tip, while, from its center, cream came
out.

———

There are a lot of flukes in the world, sudden syn-
chronicities that appear out of nowhere and fade back.
One day you meet your long-lost and very best first-
grade friend on a street in Sri Lanka, where you both
just happen to be touring. Or you find, in your city's
trash pile, the precise tin tile, with its pressed-flower
medallion and beveled edges, that is missing from your
ceiling in an otherwise perfect period home. These are
the brief, blessed moments that charm our lives, and
we know better than to count on them.

At first I figured this Prozac business was a fluke. I
mentioned the change to no one. Few had heard of
Prozac, a still brand-new medication; books and
articles about it had not yet appeared. My aloneness in
the experience only added to my sense of incredulity. I
tiptoed around for the next few days, looking left, then
right, pausing to consider. Was I still feeling OK? I

touched my head, my eyes. I stroked the lobe of my ear, feeling the skin almost impossibly soft there.

When four more days had passed and I still felt so shockingly fine, I called the Prozac Doctor. I pictured him high in the eaves of McLean. In my mind his teeth had grown whiter, his hair blacker, and light leapt out from his wooden desk.

"I'm well," I told him.

"Not yet," he said. "You only started nine days ago. It may take a month, or even more, to build up a thera-peutic blood level."

"No," I said. "I'm well." I felt a rushing joy as I spoke. "I've, I've actually never felt better."

There was a pause on the line. "I'm not sure that's possible, so fast," he said.

So fast.

—

Still today, in writing this, I doubt the accuracy of my memory. Research seems to support the notion that Prozac is a slow-acting agent, over weeks or months peeling away the thick skin of illness. My friend Sara, also on Prozac, tells me I've misrepresented the drug, at least according to her experience, which was much more along the lines of researched case studies, a gradual lifting of a dusty curtain. However, my friends

Susan and Emily, also, alas, on Prozac, say they, like me, recall a very specific moment when, for the first time, "things seemed right."

I wonder if Sara objects to my miracle-tinged description of the drug because it smacks of the illicit, puts one, maybe, in mind of heroin, which "hits" suddenly, or acid, often described as having a very definitive moment of onset. Perhaps we are uncomfortable thinking that Prozac may have properties similar to those "bad" drugs, for Prozac is supposedly not "bad," and it is not illicit, and those who take it, myself included, may dislike descriptions that suggest how close and complex is the relationship between prescribed and socially legitimized substance use and its underbelly, the syringes and tabs and little silver snifters.

Also, the effects of Prozac are probably as various as the people who ingest it. For Sara and many others, Prozac, when it works at all, works more slowly and less dramatically. I have a hunch that the initial effects of Prozac are in direct proportion to the subjective distress of the consumer. I had experienced my various psychiatric conditions as devastating. I was five and the roses were red claws. I was ten and terrified to go outside. I was twelve and grew so thin the bones turned to blades in my neck. In secret, on our wide porch, I cut myself. I knew nothing of pleasure. At fifteen, right when my life should have been growing, it warbled and shrank to the size of a hard, dark dot.

And the hospitalizations, five of them, barriers all. I used to stand on the barred-in balcony and watch the traffic move beneath me, a dog with his head out the window, a woman in sunglasses shaped like dragonfly wings. Insects hovered over the river to my left, and girls lay out on the grass in a thick glaze of sun. I could smell the coconut of Coppertone, the whiffs of warm exhaust, the dog's damp fur, and the brine of city river, but none of it belonged to me. My hospital johnny belonged to me, and the garment was blue. I have the johnny still, hanging in the back of my closet, a worn cotton smock printed with tiny white snowflakes. Sometimes I take it out. I try it on, and it is too small. The cotton ties are frayed, and there is a strange smell to it, a smell I have not known for years.

Disinfectant. Sweat. Sharp. Wet.

The pill, I noticed those first few days of our acquaintance, had no smell. It had no taste, either. It in and of itself was not a sensation, but rather the rocket to sensation, the oval opening through which I slid.

And slid. Off the barred-in balcony, down to the river; I tried it all. The air felt like flannel on my skin. And in my mind Barbar Jean came back to me, and he called me Chief, and when he held out his hands they were cupping colors. It should come as no surprise that this was so, that after years of illness my remission on that first drugged day—confusing, yes, portending loss, yes—was also a blessing, pure and simple. No, not a blessing, a redemption, both bright and blinding, heaven opening up, letting me in.

Good morning.

Those first few mornings were fairy tales, tall tales, replete with all the bent beauty of a new world. I saw a raven, an egg full of gold. I blinked and blinked again. I started to understand that, like Gretel, I might need a map, a scatter of something to mark my way, but when it comes to deciphering health there is surprisingly little help. The Judeo-Christian tradition, of which I am firmly a part, views health as a gift from God and therefore decisively good. The Western medical profession, which grew directly out of our Judeo-Christian culture, takes things one step further, claiming health is not only good but natural. After all, when you are sick, there are plenty of places (insurance willing) where you can go to get healed, but when you are healed are there any places you can go to learn not to be sick? The very idea of having to learn the landscape of health sounds vaguely ridiculous, so ensconced are so many of us in the notion that health is as organic as grass, in the right conditions growing green and freely.

Certainly some of our most influential healers have not viewed health as an alien form of beauty. Freud envisioned the human body as a rather banal hydraulic machine seeking to maintain homeostasis at all times, a humming equilibrium in which the gears and chimes of bone and brain worked harmoniously. Robert Ornstein, a neuropsychologist, calls the brain a "health maintenance organization," whose purpose is to keep thriving and balanced all the body's systems. New Age doctors like Deepak Chopra have gone even further or, perhaps, been more explicit, stating that the human animal seeks health at all costs, its entire construction geared to the maintenance of the robust.

But health, at least in my case, was not so natural, and despite its allure, I am not totally sold on its goodness either. My experience with Prozac and the kind of rushing recovery it spawned has caused me, at the risk of nostalgia, to look with favor upon the old sanatoriums and convalescent homes of the late-eighteenth and early-nineteenth centuries, halfway houses where the chronically ill, now recovering, hovered in their newfound health, tentatively trying it out, buttoning and unbuttoning, resewing the seams, until at last the new outfit seemed right. The old-fashioned convalescent home, chairs stretched by the salty sea, isolated from the world and yet close on the cusp of it, acknowledged the need for a supportive transition, moving the patient incrementally from an illness-based identity to a health-based identity, out of the hospital, not yet home, hovering, stuttering, slowly learning to speak the sanguine alphabet again.

—

If I could have learned to speak that alphabet more slowly, then maybe my story would have played out differently. Prozac did not start out for me as a dangerous drug but over the following months it sometimes became that way. There was so much I wanted to try. I, a long-term mental patient in my mid-twenties, had never been to a rock concert, had, with few exceptions and great displeasure, rarely left New England, had never been swimming at Walden Pond, had not in years eaten a meal without anxiety, taken a walk for no reason, allowed myself to sleep late, casually dated a man, or, in short, just played.

The play started out simply enough. I developed an interest in real estate magazines, especially the freebies stacked in stands along the streets. *Harmon Homes,*

Bremis's Better Buys, Century 21, Country Cottages by Val.
Back in my apartment I read them, each abbreviated
description—lvly gambrel with sunken l/r flr and e/i
kitch, C/A, C/Alrm, come see the charm!—providing
a porthole through which I swam into new spaces. I
could feel the cool air circulating inside that gambrel,
see light the color of candy pouring through the leaded-
glass windows. There were gardens, for sure, and they
contained beautiful flowers, flowers I could smell and
see, whose names both proposed and fulfilled the most
sensual of possibilities—climax marigolds and false
dragonhead, meadowsweet and hollyhocks, pink baby's
breath growing side by side with slender spikes of
salvia, which, before blooming, issued a froth of sticky
white bubbles under the little leaves.

I spent hours imagining myself inside the plethora of
houses the world suddenly made available to me. I
started going to open houses. I saw chandeliers sprout-
ing down through intricate ceiling medallions, old gas
lamps and blue vases on cream-colored windowsills. In
bathrooms I opened the double doors of medicine cabi-
nets and found evidence of sour stomachs and stress
headaches, everyday pains. I observed kitchens where
foods had been cooked, and I touched double beds with
pale yellow stains on otherwise perfectly white pillows.
At night I even dreamt of houses, expansive and gor-

geous dreams, room opening onto room, old marble garden tables, stone Cupids, quilts and spiraling stair-cases, huge glass walls and vaulted ceilings where, from the shadows, loons and peacocks called.

—

In the month that followed, I began to range farther and wider, getting reckless, hungry from all the time I'd lost to illness. I started going out late at night, prowling around by myself until two or three in the morning, standing by the edge of the city river and admiring the waxy sheen of light on the water or exploring the alleys of Boston, where broken things glittered. I felt invulnerable. Propelled by an unquenchable curiosity, I was a twenty-six-year-old with the judgment of an early adolescent. I had a special fondness for Faneuil Hall, where men and food thrived side by side. I floated up and down the cobblestoned corridors, too nervous to approach anyone but certainly not too nervous to eat. I had never before not cared about food, and now I reveled in my relaxed attitude. I didn't know when to stop. Although I had not been clinically anorexic in many years, I had always fretted about my weight. Years of this had left me alienated from my stomach's signals, and I was unaware of what it meant to be full. I remember wandering from stall to stall eating jelly beans in a sack, and dots—little sugary disks of pale yellow

and pink and blue stuck on strips of white paper—
strings of licorice, malted-milk balls, and gelato so
light it felt like foam in my throat. I tried lemon
ices and raspberry tortes and wedges of cake blistered
with nuts. I bought a frozen piña colada at an outdoor
bar—the first time I'd ever ordered from a bar—and,
feeling supremely sophisticated, I toted the frothed
concoction around, delicately sipping through a crin-
kled straw. The glass was cold, and at one point I
remember stopping and pressing it to my cheeks, my
forehead, the way my mother had a long time ago,
when I was ill and my fever needed to be brought
down.

And indeed, sometimes in the midst of this newness,
this rampant exploration, my body tanked on sugar and
dough, I wanted to cry. I often, inexplicably, felt this
way while watching the Faneuil Hall magician, a bril-
liant performer with straw-blond hair and a black top
hat, with whom I promptly fell in love. This was a magician who knew his craft, who could make flowers
blossom from silk swatches and birds flock from his fist.
Night after night I watched him, and as the summer
went by his acts got increasingly complex and wonderful and bizarre, drawing ever larger crowds. One
night when I went to see him he had a female assistant
with him, and he put her in a box. He brandished a

sword, its blade red in the lamplight. The assistant's head jutted out one end of the box, her feet the other. She was wearing tiny black pumps, and her hair poured onto the pavement. He cut her in half, very slowly, very lovingly, smiling down at her while she smiled up at him. He separated her parts, walked between them to underscore their bifurcation, and then, with a flourish and a whoop, jammed her back together so she jumped out of the box, whole and unharmed. They kissed. I watched, mesmerized. The crowd clapped and clapped. I clapped too, but I was not sure what for. When I looked up, the lights of the marketplace were spinning; the odors of hot dogs and pizza were strong, too strong.

He had a kitten with him then, this magician, a little tiger-striped thing that he dangled by the scruff of its neck and plunged into a tub of water. The crowd gasped and fell silent. We could see the animal struggling, or, rather, see his hand holding something frantic down, and down, and down. I felt myself falling. Two minutes passed. Then three. Then four. The struggling stopped. He whooped again, and pulled the same kitten, completely dry and thrivingly alive, from the bucket of water. The world, apparently, was full of illusion, and what was real was not real. I was lost and found, and in the finding still more lost.

"Now," he said, "for my finest act." He scanned the

crowd that had grown, by now, to hundreds. "I need a volunteer."

No one volunteered.

"Contrary to all appearances," he said, "I am a loving man. I won't hurt you. The whole point of my show is to demonstrate the illusory nature of evil. You see?" He smiled. He had a charming smile, and some people popped up their hands, most of them girls with blond or brown ponytails and perfect summer tans.

"I cannot choose," he said, "from such a small sample. I need a genuine response, lots of volunteers. Put up your hands, people. Put up your hands."

"Put up your hands, people, put up your hands," the assistant called, clapping her own tiny white hands with painted nails. Some men, now, put up their hands, and then a field of hands flourished.

The magician looked around. I did not put up my hand, which is probably why he chose me. Or perhaps he had seen me standing there, night after night, a girl/woman on the edge of awkwardness and excitement. "You," he said to me. "You are the one."

I put my hand to my chest and mouthed *me?*

"Yes, you," he said. "I can see you have the mystical sort of temperament this act needs in order to, shall we say, fly. Come into the center now. Come come."

I went into the center, and he placed a lightbulb in

my hand. His assistant walked around with a silver snuffer dousing all the gas lamps and candles surrounding his pavement stage. "Hold your palm very still," he said to me. "Hold your palm very still, and think of what it is you most want."

I closed my eyes and thought. I held my palm as still as I could. What was it I wanted? The press of possibilities? The planets, so many, too many, strewn in the sky? The openness of new space, new skin, me and not me, foreign and frightening, lost and found? Where was I? Who was I? I did not know what I wanted.

I heard a drawn-out "oooh" from the crowd. I felt something lift from my palm. "And open your eyes," the magician whispered to me, leaning down close, his lips at my ear.

I opened my eyes and saw the lightbulb maybe five feet above me, lit up, a detached and glowing yellow sphere, a lost and lovely shape hovering. It was a head without a body, an unmoored mind. "You've done it," he said. "She's done it," he shouted, and it was a few moments before I realized the crowd, that crowd, clapped for me.

—

At home, later on that night, I took off my clothes and looked at myself. My skin had browned from the summer sun. My eyes were clear as newly washed windows. I was the picture of health, as though I had finally come into the body meant for me, the body that had been with me even before birth, its shape hovering in the unformed fetus, fleshing out, fleshing out.

I felt at home in this body. The curiosities and energies that had always been rightfully mine were finally taking their place. This must be what people mean when they say, "Prozac helped me become the person I was meant to be."

And yet for me it was not that simple. My personality, yes, had always consisted of suppressed energies and curiosities, but also of depressions, echoing intensities, drivenness that tipped into pain. With the exception of the counting and touching obsessions, which I was only too happy to be rid of, I missed these things, or parts of them anyway, for they were as familiar to me as dense fog and drizzle, which has its own sort of lonely beauty, as does a desert or the most mournful of music.

Looking in the mirror, I touched my bronzed shoulders and nose with its sunny saddle of freckles. I thought of the lightbulb, loosed, and when I pictured it, it was floating still, far from the magician's black bag, floating over a dark field and then the moving marble of the Atlantic Ocean, searching for its socket, pulsing and bright.

In the past, I had always recorded images that were odd or moving to me in my journal. My methods, perhaps, were a bit odd. When I wrote, it was not from "me," but from eight people I pictured living inside of me, eight people who had kept me company for more years than I can remember. While I knew these people were not "real," while I could say, *"They are figments in my mind,"* I still experienced them as flesh, heard them, felt them—three men who taunted me, three nine-year-olds, a girl trapped in a glass case, and a blue baby, sometimes dead, sometimes dying. These eight beings comprised my core. I knew myself by knowing them— the blue baby's craving for comfort, the glassed-in girl's high-pitched anxiety, her desire for freedom clashing with her need for the airless perfection of a crystal world.

Blue Baby was the one who usually had the most interesting things to say to me. When it spoke, I went into a light trance, my pen moving as if of its own accord, and when it was finished speaking, I felt as though I'd visited a place too intense to be anything but real. Here is an example, something Blue Baby wrote to me years before I started Prozac.

Mother of many
Watch your children play

Hightailing across a field, leaving you
With nothing but a spray of snow.
So cup your hands and try to catch all that's left
Of your children.

The water takes us in and as we sink
Our snowsuits shine beneath the lake's
Ice lens. We cry from below
Bubbles rise and in the woods creeks weep
Go on, get down on your knees, look for
A buckle or a bit of mitten. Ear to the ground
Can't you hear our whispers and waterlogged dreams?
At night we call you
Does it comfort you to think that death came gracefully
That we danced our way down?

All that winter we skated figure eights
Against a sky so blue
It should have been an omen
So when the ice opened to admit us
Shouldn't you have heard it crack?
Don't let yourself imagine how the fish must nibble
How our dresses fill and float

Go on, float to us
Quiet in the hallway. Slipperless

Your feet should freeze
Out across the field, eyes wild from the wind
In your head. Fill your apron with stones
Go now
Over the ice. And when it opens
To admit you, don't look back
Have no second thoughts
You will be like a long lost child
Going home

Now, back in my apartment, I picked up my pen and opened my journal. I closed my eyes, bent over the page, and waited. I said *yes* to myself, which in the past had been the signal for Blue Baby to emerge and speak with me. Now I heard silence.

Yes. Hello.

Nothing.

Yes, hello.

Maybe a slight stir, a quickening that faded fast.

I kept my eyes closed. And then I could see them all down there, Blue Baby curled, the girl in the glass case biting at her nails. And then I could hear them down there, snatches of sentences I transcribed on paper, but the words felt dull, dead. A bright layer separated me from them, and as I sensed correctly at the time, the barrier would remain as a perpetual part of my Prozac career. That night I tried again and again. Calling. *Shhh.* Calling. *Shhh.* The air swirled. Something flapped and faded.

I finally fell into a troubled sleep, and I woke with fear. Monday morning. Writing had always been essential to me, not the academic stuff of school, but the looser and loftier stuff of stories and poems. I called the Prozac Doctor.

"I feel weird," I said.

"Weird," he repeated. "Like how?"

I paused, struggling to find the words. "I'm worried."

"Of course you're worried," he said. "You're an obsessive. Obsessives worry."

"No," I said. "I'm not obsessively worrying. I'm worrying unobsessively about the medication. Do you think it can take away your creativity?"

"There have been no studies on that question," the Prozac Doctor said. "But I doubt it. I certainly wouldn't worry about it."

"I don't feel like me," I said. "I mean, I feel more like me in some ways and less like me in others. I'm scared. I'm really worried," I said, my voice rising with the memory of silence, company I could not reach.

"I hear that," he said. "Your worry indicates the presence of pathology. We should think about upping your dose."

He told me to take two capsules a day instead of one, which, at first, I didn't do. In fact, I was thinking of stopping the Prozac altogether, torn between my desire for my old self and my enthusiasm for the new. I was concerned that Prozac, and the health it spawned, could take away not only my creativity but my very identity. And the answer to that—although there had been "no studies"—was a certain yes. I was a different person now, both more and less like me, fulfilling one possibility while swerving from another. There is loss in that swerving. And my experience on Prozac showed me how few there are who understand that loss or are prepared for its expression.

The work of the psychiatrist Arthur Kleinman focuses on the subjective meanings of illness. He calls illness, or suffering, a narrative, which, at its best, concatenates a coherent story of self. Symptoms and pain take on value as they become symbols referring to something larger than themselves. The cancer patient must make of her pain *this* or *that*. The schizophrenic sees his pain, perhaps, as stories sent by gods and devils, and as such the stories are rich in reverberations. Illness, according to Kleinman, is more than a set of symptoms, over the long term transforming itself into the hows and whys and ways of being.

Having lived with chronic depression, a high-pitched panic, and a host of other psychiatric symptoms since my earliest years, I had made for myself an illness identity, a story of self that had illness as its main motive. I did not sleep well because I was ill. I cut myself because I was ill. Illness, for me, had been the explanatory model on which my being was based. Since I had spent much time in mental hospitals, illness had also been something I'd learned, like a skill, like spelling. From Rosie and Katie I had acquired ever new and niftier ways of cutting myself, admiring the ruby zippers that tracked these girls' arms. From Ann I'd learned anxiety's different positions and sounds, its jagged breaths and sweat. I knew medication's spectrum, colored liquid Thorazine, the melted sky of Stelazine, lavender Halcions and Ativans scattered like snowflakes on a steel tray. Illness was language as well as color; I knew a secret special language with words like *sharps* and *checks* and *rounds,* and then the longer, arcane phrases and words that every patient picks up—*trichotillomania* and *waxy flexibility, Munchhausen's* and *borderlines*—the most mysterious word of all, suggesting the line of the horizon, a flat world, a ship tipping over into star-filled night.

And now, gone. I had tipped over, stepped over the border into health. There was no more depression, which had felt like the stifling yet oddly comforting weight of a woolen blanket, or anxiety, which lent a certain fluorescence to things, or voices, which had always been there, sometimes louder, sometimes softer, some North Star of sound in the night.

—

A few days later I had my first follow-up appointment with the Prozac Doctor. His office was just as I remembered it, large, gracious, a plush rug on the floor. Added to his Prozac paraphernalia was a three-dimensional model of a plastic synapse showing how the drug worked. The synapse, which looked like one of those Krazy Straws, all looped and bent, was bright pink, and its tip ended in a dish, labeled the synaptic cleft, where turquoise liquid, simulating serotonin, pooled. He demonstrated for me. By pushing a button on the right, he made the synapse twitch, sucking up the serotonin at a brisk clip. "The obsessive brain," he said, nodding toward me. When he pushed the button on the left, however, the synapse slowed down its sucking, allowing the serotonin to remain lapping in its gap.

"By allowing the serotonin to remain for longer periods of time in the synaptic cleft," he said, "Prozac can alter mood and, it appears, diminish, if not eradicate, OCD."

"But what else does it diminish or eradicate?" I asked.

"You are still worried," he said to me, trying to act like a therapist, which was not at all in his nature. Still, I appreciated the effort.

"Yes," I said. I was too embarrassed to tell him about the eight people in me. "I'm still feeling . . . off. Off in a good way, I think, but—"

"Symptoms," the Prozac Doctor said to me. "Let's review your anxiety symptoms. Obsessive thoughts?"

"Very few," I said.

"Would you say a sixty percent reduction?"

"Eighty, ninety, maybe even ninety-five."

"Excellent," the Prozac Doctor said. "A marvelous response. Depression?"

"Absolutely none," I said. "Except—"

"Except what? Are you sleeping well?"

"Yes."

"Concentration?"

"I can read faster than I could before, and my thinking's clear."

"Eating?"

"A lot," I said.

At this he looked concerned. He sat back in his chair

and folded his arms across his crisp suit. He knew about my history of eating disorders. "Binging?" he asked.

"No," I said. "I'm not binging. It's not compulsive. I'm just not so afraid of getting fat. I don't think I will get fat, even though I guess I've gained. I'm just sampling a lot of foods I never allowed myself to try before."

"Purging?" he said, looking straight at me.

I shook my head no.

"Well," he said, steepling his fingertips and staring up at the ceiling. "It seems Prozac has made you almost completely symptom-free. You have had a beautiful response to it. Consider yourself lucky."

—

I left. I stepped outside his office and onto the grounds of McLean, a large hospital where I felt, not surprisingly, at ease. In the distance a white-haired woman drifted across the tended lawn. Two doctors wheeled a machine into a small door on the side of a brick building. When I looked up, I could see the windows of the wards, the cool shadows of people moving in a sealed and special world.

I slipped into the hospital's medical library, where, supposedly, only doctors and nurses were allowed to go. The woman at the front desk, busy writing something, didn't see me, and before she looked up, I

whisked myself into the shady stacks. Dust motes
spun in the rafters above me. An air conditioner
hummed, hummed like the humidifier had, long ago, in
my childhood sickroom. There had been my mother,
and stories from a silver book, the heat of fever like
love between us.

Now I looked up at the titles of the books. My eyes
burned, and when I looked down I imagined a child
standing before me, her hair white-blond, her expression serious. She seemed to stand in her own circle of
sun. She seemed to want something from me, maybe a
book out of reach, an answer to a question. She was a
child, I knew, real and not real, an intimate expression
of my faded insides, which she took with her when she
left, dazzling and dissolving into the high ceiling, the
vaulted ceiling of some new house, where loons and
peacocks called.

—

Prozac, at least in my case, did not eliminate worry;
rather, it shortened its life span so my bouts of fretting
over the drug were rather rapidly replaced by longer
bouts of cheer. And confidence. In the weeks that followed I learned to drink lattes while reading Rabelais. I
made some friends at an outdoor café—Molly, Car-
away, Pamela. Readers of *The Nation* and scoffers at
Newsweek, they took me with them to Harvard Yard,

where I recited impromptu poetry for them at the foot of a statue, and then to a clothing store called Oona's, where we bought used leather coats and crushed-velvet skirts. I found a book about résumé writing, and for the first time in my life I turned to the professional section in the paper's Help Wanted ads. Why should I be a waitress, as I had been in the past? Why should I cut deli behind the counter at Formaggio's? That I had no skills except in these areas seemed a minor problem. The passages in my brain were clear of all congestion. I could learn anything. I could convince anyone. I could lie.

I started to send to schools a résumé I had written— I thought I might like to try teaching—on which I claimed phantom jobs in distant states as a humanities researcher, a teen-suicide counselor, and finally an English instructor at a private academy, where I pictured frail dogwoods growing by a black lacy fence. The résumé remains, to date, one of my finest pieces of fiction. Only days after having sent it out, I got several requests for interviews and, not long after that, an actual job offer at a literacy center. I am proud and ashamed of that résumé, for it shows the kind of drunk doggedness you sometimes need in order to thrive in a competitive world. I had it printed on ivory paper, a weave thick enough to soak up the stains of deceit.

And then one evening, shortly before accepting my new job offer, I dressed for my first concert ever. An old high school buddy had gotten us tickets to see Michelle Shocked. I had been on the medication, altogether, for not more than two months. I put on black leggings and a black tunic and a choker of red around my neck, and although I intended this costume to express my adventurousness, now I see it also as a sign of what I felt inside, the choker shining like a slash on my neck.

Now that I was a Prozac person, I owned a good bit of makeup, which I had bought at the CVS, standing by mirrors and furtively applying cherry balm and frosty pink. That evening I wore my makeup too, and I slung an army knapsack over my shoulder.

I had never seen such a crowd in love, and it moved me even further beyond myself, up and out. When Michelle Shocked came onto the stage, thousands surged forward, flicking lighters in the air. All around me, bodies moved, and I had to move too, because I was a part of something larger. Michelle crooned out ballads about ice and red clay roads, about high skies and dead friends, and I trembled. The man next to me trembled. He took my hand and had me move left, now right, now out of the aisle and up close to the stage, the music pouring. And then it was over.

"My name," he said, speaking into the sudden silence, his accent Israeli, "is Yehuda."

"Yehuda," I thought, swooning stupidly. Joshua, the name of the biblical boy who fought the lions, the heroic man who overcame evil. Such a man could not hurt me. Such a man could only help me. And he was handsome to boot, dark eyes, dark curly hair, broad in all the right ways.

"Lauren," I said, looking down at the floor.

He was very forward, that Yehuda. He put his hand right under my chin and tipped it up, so I was staring straight into his oh-so-sincere eyes. "I am new to this country," he said. "Visiting for a few weeks. I am planning to move here next year. Will you show me around?"

"Yes," I said. *Moving here,* I thought. *Handsome,* I thought. *Jewish,* I thought.

He pulled a bandanna out of his baggy pants and wiped his forehead. Saturday night, muggy, not too late. "I would like to go swimming," he said. "I have heard there are some very good swimming places, not too far."

My friend, at this point, had found me in the crowd. "Time to go," she said.

"I'll call you later," I said to her. "This is Yehuda. We're going swimming."

She narrowed her eyes and looked at me. "Swimming, huh?" She bent close to me. "You're sure that's what you want?"

Yehuda was staring at us. She looked from him to me. "Swimming, huh?" she said again, her voice full of portent. "Aren't you just getting over strep?"

"I'm fine," I said. And, indeed, I did feel fine, quite confident all would be well. I pulled her aside. "He's actually a friend. An old cousin of mine," I lied. "It's amazing we met here, family from Israel."

"Yehuda is your cousin," she repeated. "What other cousins do you have, maybe some from Afghanistan, Egypt, Africa? A real international family."

I had a brief image, then, of the eight people inside me, north of my neck, south of my stomach, a muffled population, a distant planet.

"He's the only cousin I have," I said, and for a second I believed it.

—

Cousin Yehuda had a nice little rental car, a spiffy red thing with a convertible top. He was very polite, ushering me out of the concert hall ahead of him, suavely opening doors and taking my elbow to cross the street. As soon as we had buckled into his vehicle, though, he announced that the night air had cooled him, and he no longer felt like swimming. From his glove compartment he pulled out a tour book, thumbed through it, and announced he would like to visit Boston's famous deer park.

"Boston's famous deer park?" I repeated. I'd lived in Boston all my life and had never heard of such a thing.

He put the tour book in my lap, and sure enough, there it was, in a close-by suburb, open round the clock, in all seasons, described in lush and loving terms, acres of trees, fawns springing over moss while the city skyline glowed in the distance.

"OK," I said, basically agreeing to drive into a forest with a strange six-foot man, one of my dumber decisions, informed by the off-kilteredness that was health to me.

We arrived there in less than twenty minutes. Evergreens spiked into the air. Through the dense darkness I could see the hovering shapes of the trees, their roots breaking the earth like the tendons showing through skin. Something moist and furry brushed my knee. Insects rose from rotting logs. He held my hand, this Joshua who beat the beasts, this king and cousin, he took my hand and led me into the wild.

My heart was paddling, half from fear, half from excitement. This was life, yes. Here I was, yes. Something flapped above me, a taut wing with a reddish membrane stretched over piping of bone. "Bats," Yehuda announced calmly.

My eyes adjusting to the darkness, I could see better now. I could see bats soaring beneath the trees. I could see the craggy cliff that was this man's face, jutting nose, rocky chin, the steep slopes of his Sephardic cheeks. I didn't think he would hurt me. After all, he came from Israel, and as he'd told me while we stood on the concert floor, he'd been in the army. To a Jewish girl raised by fiercely Zionist parents, that fact made it all seem safe. He was one of the men I'd watched on television as a child. He had rescued the athletes at Munich; he had personally guarded the Golan Heights, folding victims of terrorist attacks into his warm bulk.

And, like all army men, he was more a doer than a talker. As soon as we reached a clearing, he didn't waste much time swooping me into his arms like I was a victim myself, laying me down on the forest floor, where the worms were.

"Wait a minute," I said, pushing him off me.

"OK," he said, sitting up. I guess he took me quite literally. He peered at his watch, and after what seemed like precisely a minute had gone by, he descended again, my cousin Yehuda. He unbuttoned my tunic and managed to finagle a breast.

"No. No. Wait a minute," I said, and this time I scuttled away from him.

"OK," he said in the same good-natured voice. He held up his hands in a protest of innocence and then casually slung one arm around my shoulder. We sat in silence. I could feel the forest encroaching from all sides, the breaths of a million beasts, insects working the earth, dragging and devouring.

I shuddered, and Yehuda pulled me closer, a gesture both threatening and comforting, locking me in. "The moon," he said softly, looking up through the trees, "is complete."

Indeed, it was a full moon, large and a little sickly-looking. I myself felt a bit sick now, like I might be getting that strep my friend had mentioned.

"I have a sore throat," I announced, a comment that makes such perfect sense, for illness had always been both my escape and my means of seduction, the heat between my mother and me.

The Israeli, as though on cue, turned to me. He looked straight at me, his pupils deep as inkwells. As though he had known me forever, he started to stroke my throat, up and down, up and down, long hypnotizing movements, like a lullaby. He didn't push me down or fumble with my buttons, just stroked and stroked, allowing me to open at my own pace. I kissed him first.

I think he could sense my fear. He made love to me like I was a virgin, very delicately. The whole time I felt there and not there. I felt waves of fear and pleasure. My body responded, rising to his touch. However, my mind felt detached, and while there was warmth there was also ice, wedging up between us, within me. I had little experience with sex. My one long-term relationship in college had coincided with my most severe period of anorexia. The last time I'd made love I'd weighed ninety pounds, a woman without a period, a woman all bone and brain, no flesh. This flesh was new to me. Deep in my body, eggs ripened and dropped. Snakes slid on the ground. I imagined deer came forward, hundreds of them, thousands of them watching us with wet and ghostly eyes. Something moaned. Inside me an organ I'd never felt before reddened and stretched. This was new. Pleasure was new. He was new. I was making love not to one stranger but to two.

—

He dropped me off in front of my apartment building, and only once I was inside did I realize I was shaking.

What from? A narrow escape? The peak of pleasure? A potential rape? A love?

The image of deer kept coming back to me. We hadn't seen any, but I had felt them, their hot breath and rocking canters, their antlers, covered with fuzz.

And when I peeled off my clothes, I saw scat on the back of them, and three hairs from the finest hide.

—

Three days passed, my breasts filled, and still my period didn't come. I pressed at my stomach, and whenever liquid slid from me, I rushed to the bathroom to peer. Nothing.

But inside, everything. Inside, things puffed and leaked and ripened in lumps. I felt a little fish swimming, a speckled tadpole turning, and turning again.

Terror. I remembered Yehuda, only now without complexity. Now he was purely bad, a man immersed in bloodied bodies, a man with weapons he'd let loose in me, this baby a blade. As for sex, well, sex was sweet but clearly dangerous, and you could lose yourself in it, if you had not already lost yourself outside of it, sucking down Prozac, those plump little green-and-cream-colored spheres.

I let a week go by, and then I took myself to a women's health clinic in Brookline. I was so convinced I was pregnant that I wanted to schedule an abortion before I'd even had a test. "You're putting the cart before the horse," the assistant said, and wouldn't comply.

In a small room with potholders on stirrups and a poster of Monet's water lilies on the ceiling, which women were meant to stare at while doctors did things to them, I got my blood taken. Then they put my blood into a little blender and whipped it up. I kept having to run to the bathroom, I was so nervous. AIDS had not even crossed my mind, only pregnancy. I figured Israelis didn't have AIDS.

"OK," the nurse said, motioning me from the waiting room, where they had sent me while the test was brewing. I tipped back into the examining room.

"Negative," the doctor said.

Bliss. I loved the Israeli all over again. And what fun that night now seemed, with all those deer.

"I need some birth control," I said to him. "I need a diaphragm." Actually, I wasn't planning to sleep with anybody. The Israeli had gone back home and was probably right now flying in a jet over the desert. But still. Just in case.

"Let's get you fitted," he said. I liked the idea of a diaphragm. I pictured its small rubber cap snapped over my cervix, containing me, covering me while I exposed my skin.

The doctor, who was Russian and who was wearing a name tag that said BORIS YAZLOVIAN, put on his gloves and then checked me. His fingers in me hurt a bit, that organ reddening and stretching. I winced.

"Hmmm," he said. "Is there pain?"

"Yes," I said. "A little."

I was familiar with that particular pain. Anytime I'd had intercourse, there had always been a sting and stretch if the man moved in a certain way. I hadn't thought to check it out, just figured it was one of my womanly perks, like a period. After all, I'd never totally reconciled myself to the idea of someone sticking something inside of me, in my rawest part. Of course, along with pleasure, it should hurt a little.

The doctor lowered his head between my legs, and then there was more pain. "Excuse me," I said.

He bobbed back up. His face was flushed, a man who had just made a mighty discovery. "You," he said in his thick Russian accent, "you are still a virgin."

"Am not," I said, sounding like an eighth-grader. I was offended. After all, since I'd been on Prozac, I was a woman of the world. Lightbulbs lifted from me, men entered me, I rode on the ridged backs of stags.

"Yes, you are," he repeated. "Even though you are a sexually active twenty-six-year-old, you are still, medically speaking, a virgin."

And then he explained to me how I had an unusual hymen, O-shaped and intact, very stretched but not quite clipped. A tough little hymen, he said, a stubborn, grisly circle of skin that would bend but not break, and that was responsible for the occasional pain.

"We should take care of it," he said, and I swear I saw a glint in his eye. "It's a simple medical procedure. A local anesthetic, snip, and the end."

But I was perfectly fine with my hymen the way it was.

"Oh, no," he said. "It's not normal."

I pictured my hymen, a red wedge within me, something, through all my Prozac adventures, that had stayed the same, sealed and safe. Deep in my vagina I had my own little locked hospital room.

"We should cut it open," he said. "It's not feasible for childbirth, and continued pain during intercourse could cause . . ." He paused.

"Could cause what?" I said.

"Psychological difficulties," he said, lowering his voice. "You are a healthy young woman. No need to take a risk like that."

I smiled to myself. "We wouldn't want psychological difficulties," I said to him. I pictured him cutting, the door opening, Blue Baby, Glassed-In Girl tumbling out of me, birthed from me, severed and separate.

"In five minutes it will be over," he said, calling in a nurse, not waiting for me to acquiesce. In the name of health, I let him lead. A shot of Novocain, and my insides hummed and numbed. The scissors were tiny, like cuticle clippers. I felt not a thing. I heard a crisp *snap*. In that moment the last cords to my old self, my sick self, were cut. I thought of the pictures I'd seen as a child, astronauts floating around a foreign moon, all space silent.

I started to cry. At first I cried lightly, so the nurse and doctor did not notice. As they wheeled me down the hall, though, I started to cry harder, as though there had been a hymen in my throat as well and now that it was gone the grief of health rose up and ran out.

The corridor was narrow. White lights burned above. We passed what must have been a vacuum aspirator machine, and it was full of fresh contents, glinting and salty. Blue Baby.

I closed my eyes. I put my hands over my emptied stomach. The Novocain was wearing off now, and my birth canal buzzed, like there was a bee caught in there, like you sometimes find a bee in an abandoned room, buzzing and buzzing amid the dusty furniture.

The nurses in the recovery room, where I was placed, were so kind. The room was full of women in various stages of anesthesia, and all of them, I think, had just had abortions. Some lay with their bruised-looking lids closed; others struggled to sit up; one woman moaned, and a nurse held a cup of ginger ale to her lips.

I kept crying, freely now, having finally arrived at a place made just for grief. I thought of the hospital, a nurse named Iris, the luscious look of red medicine in a plastic cup, the grayness of depression, the edge of anxiety, both of which had given me my voice, the people I'd lost, all cords cut. "It's OK, dear," a nurse said to me, coming over to stroke my hair. I'm sure she thought I was recovering from an abortion, and in a way she was right. Girl gone. Blue Baby gone. "It will all seem better soon," she said. "We won't have you leave until you're ready."

Until I was ready. No one, in my Prozac career, had yet said that to me. I had arrived at my convalescent home, this brief respite in a recovery room. I lay back in the seat. I let her hand smooth my brow. She had pale lipstick on, and she had beautiful skin. The sun coming in through the window sifted through her hair, making the blondness glow gold. Maybe, this mother, she would read me a story. Maybe she would bring me tea and toast. Maybe she would stay until the heat passed, and then—I could see it—she would help me stand. And she would walk me forward, a bit like a bride or a very old lady, past the golf bags and French books and girlhood's privileged pressures, past the country clubs and test scores, and into a place where new animals dwelled—deer and men, fire and music— a world I might learn to live in. A world I might learn to love.

2. Comment briefly on patient's family of origin. Was there physical or sexual abuse? Neglect? Was patient victim, witness, perpetrator? Please specify and describe immediate family members with significant histories of mental illness and/or substance abuse.

Patient reports sig. history of mental illness in family of origin. Father dysthymic. Mother's behavior points to possible Axis II diagnosis, with secondary diagnosis of agitated—

Adrenaline is a drug too. In our family we were always high on it. I had a red rush in my veins, a hummingbird in my head. The phones were ringing. The butcher brought the wrong cut of meat. The Tiffany chandelier fell down. Any day now the Nazis could come back. Oh my God. Oh my God.

When I was eleven years old and my parents' marriage was definitely dissolving, my mother began cutting Holocaust crime stories out of the newspaper. There was the story of the scalpel; the rape of the Polish girl. Men came one day and installed not only an alarm system but a series of panic buttons that would blare if pushed. The panic buttons were spaced thirteen feet apart on each and every wall, drilled into the house's supporting studs. From then on, in my mind, it was not the studs but our alarm that held up the house.

The first time I ever went into the hospital, at age fourteen, I was surprised to see the same panic buttons on the desk of every doctor and social worker. I didn't understand why there were panic buttons in the professional offices but not in the patients' rooms. The discrepancy confused me. So many things confused me. In a life of constant crisis, the obvious often passed me by—how many inches there were in a foot, how to set a simple alarm clock, the kind that does not shriek to the police but slowly sings you out of sleep.

It took me a few days to realize why staff had the panic buttons and we didn't. In the hospital, a patient named Gerry needed four-point restraints. Louisa screamed and *kicked. I was one of them. Finally, the danger was no longer outside of me but inside of me. The danger was myself. Bright knife of my body. Like all things in my life, this was not a revelation in a minor key. It was operatic, intense, a sudden wrench of sense. I could not be wounded because I was now the weapon.*

October 15

I f Prozac were a sport, it might be like parachuting. A door opens, and a strong suck of wind takes you into the sky. Out there you fall fast, with a whoop and a gasp. Then comes the moment when you fumble for the rip cord, pull, and the red canopy, rippled as the surface of a human brain, opens above you. You stop falling and start, at last, to float.

I am floating now.

Nearly six months have gone by since I started this drug, and I have at last found my rip cord, which is not, by the way, the same as having found the ground.

Slowly, though, I am orienting myself to the landscape beneath my dangling feet. Things are not as wild or as tipsy as they were before. No more late-night

feasts at Faneuil Hall. No more rendezvous with
Mediterranean men. Prozac and I are growing up
together, and it is a bit of a blessing, a bit of a pity.

For instance, I have a literacy job—congratula-
tions—and the head teacher *likes* me. I make more than
minimum, which allows me to buy some snappy professional clothes, very blue and tailored. I have made
three new friends, none of whom know anything about
my past. Like a parachuter, I see how I can sculpt my
direction by small shifts in weight. I lean to the right
and paddle above a fenced-in yard, where a family is
grilling hot dogs. Will I someday have a family? How
odd to think I might wind up *conventional*. Sometimes,
up here in the sky, I sing lullabies to myself. I watch my
medicated self drift down, and down, fearful of and
longing for the level ground.

December 3

Sometimes, I guess, often, I guess, I'm more fearful
than longing. I went to see Koskava today and told him I
wanted off. Out. Kaput. Finished. "What seems to be
the problem?" he asked. "Look," I said. "I don't know if
you'll understand this, but life's become too good.
Prozac is a drug you should take before you go on vacation, like to the Caribbean. They should sell this stuff in
the CVS, along with Coppertone and beach thongs. I

feel so damn relaxed. I can't get anything really *creative* done in this state."

"And what, may I ask," he said, folding his elegant hands and leaning back in his seat, "did you get done in your prior state? If you don't mind my being so direct."

"Well," I said.

"Well," he said, jumping right in, "you are not getting as many crises done. You are not accomplishing as many hospitalizations. You are not accomplishing as much unemployment, given that you report to me you have, for the first time, a steady job as a teacher."

"But," I said, "now that I am well I haven't written a story or poem in six months. And worse, it doesn't even bother me that I haven't. I am only bothered by not being bothered. I found myself reading *Glamour* the other day, and I now enjoy shopping at Ann Taylor, which is pretty pitiful because, I'll tell you, it goes against my sense of social—"

"So go off," he said, suddenly interrupting me. He took his prescription pad then, picked it up from where it lay on his desk, and dropped it into his drawer. "No script," he said. "No script today."

Inside me I felt something seize and recede and reach, all at once.

"You," I said, suddenly furious and clear in a way I had never been before. "You are misusing your power."

"Research indicates," he said, "that Prozac helps people become more assertive in their daily interactions. Perhaps," he said, "assertiveness is something you are accomplishing now."

I shrugged. I wasn't thinking about anything anymore, except that script pad, locked away from me, the whisper of wood as he closed the drawer.

"Six months," I said. "I'll stay on this stuff for another six months, but then, I swear it, I'm through."

"Sixty milligrams," he wrote in red pen, the pad back out. "BID. X3." He handed me the piece of paper. I folded it into tiny squares and shoved it in my knapsack. Later on, when I unfolded it, I felt like I was unwrapping a tiny present, or a plea, something slipped inside the Wailing Wall, written in a language I could little understand.

December 4

There are so many things in this new state called sanity that I'm having to learn to understand and to do. For instance, the alarm clock. It's gunmetal gray, with square black buttons and a stern-looking digital display. I've never had to use an alarm clock before. In the hospital, nurses woke you. Outside of the hospital, well, what person would ever need an alarm clock when the inner bells are buzzing, when the tiniest noise is a tear in the weave of sleep? My eyes used to jerk open at five, six, seven in the morning, and I'd greet the day like an anxious athlete, all sweat and pound. Now I'm a cat. My slumbers are intense and stretched. A small sun inside my belly sends waves of perpetual warmth. I practically purr, and I find that despicable. The hours of the early morning, when I used to get my reading writing worrying nattering fraying fumbling done, are gone. There is an emptiness here. I cannot rouse myself for work without an outer bell, a plastic thing, a little zing from Lechmere's.

The alarm clock. From Lechmere's. I took it out of its box and studied it. How to set it? How to make it sing? It's not an especially unusual alarm clock; I've seen these sorts around on many a nightstand before. Now, though, it is mine, a new time. The instructions were a series of arrows and pictures. I tried setting it, but no matter what I did, it wouldn't buzz. I pushed this in and pulled that out. I shook it. I sniffed it. I pressed it and probed it. It was a corpse of a clock. Either that or, more likely, I was a corpse of a human, unlearned in the basic tasks. Finally, I carried it to the apartment upstairs. Extremely embarrassing. Excuse me. I'm having some trouble with time. I am an idiot. I need you.

"Oh," she said, peering at me through the crack in her doorway, then opening the door wider. She had fat curlers tucked beneath an aqua scarf. She was hardly a worldly woman. She took the clock, turned it on its tush and fiddled with a few things down there, and handed it back to me, all in the space of a few seconds. "That should do it," she said, looking at me oddly.

"Look," I wanted to say. "While you've been involved with cooking your chickens and buying toothpaste, I have been struggling with the grand and deep darkness. I am a philosopher, you, a mere technician."

But of course that's the statement of a snob. And even if it were true, it was the truth of the past, not the present. I'm not experiencing much grand dense darkness these days. I'm in the daily light, slowly learning to see its spectrum.

December 6, Morning

Actually, it's not a question of eyes, but of ears. In tenth-grade biology, I remember, we studied the parts of the human ear—hammer, anvil, stirrup, three tiny bones calibrated to catch and quiver with even the slightest sounds. The conch-shaped cochlea, filled with liquid, which I always imagined was blue and tepid to the touch. The entire human ear is designed like a cup, the outer rim holding in echoes, whispers, random snaps and flutters. But what, I would like to ask our tenth-grade biology teacher now, but what parts of the ear, the head, the human soul, are designed to decode silence? To make sense of the great hush? It seems to me we are creatures designed to hear relentlessly, that the slightest empty space we fill with wind, with the thief's tiptoes, or the ticking of snow as it falls against the glass pane late into the night.

This is the real problem with Prozac. As I stay on it longer and its initial euphoria wears off, I am discovering that, like a pair of parentheses, it brackets back the noisy numbness, the staccato pricks of panic. Prozac is Zen medicine, and taking it, I find myself a Zen novitiate, a Trappist oblate, trying to learn some spiritual tradition I have no knack for. Because, surely, there must be something sacred in the quiet quotidian that illness has caused me to miss.

This is what I meant to tell Koskava the other day. This is what I mean to say. In the long run, the cure called Prozac doesn't fill your mind so much as empty it of its contents and then leave you, like a pitcher, waiting to be filled.

December 6, Evening

I sat down to write in this journal and then decided I was hungry. I got up to get an apple. I pulled it from the kitchen crisper and polished it slowly on my shirt. I eased into a kitchen chair and put my feet up on the table. I bit in. The skin popped beneath the pressure of my teeth, and juice dribbled down my chin. Is this undignified or delightful? Slothful or sensual? Whom was I betraying?

In all the years I lived at home, I never saw my mother in such a posture. I never saw her spine waver, or the cleft beneath her mouth shine with the grease of meat or the wetness of fresh fruit. Once I did see her naked, in the shower, her body wrapped in a muff of steam, her angles temporarily softened, her breasts like fish floating on white foam. That image has stayed with me forever, a small and private possibility I keep to myself, in the corner of my mind, at the edge of every nighttime dream.

But she was not a woman of steam and showers. She was a woman whose scalp prickled with manic intensity. She was a woman who worked relentlessly—never for money; my father did that—who polished her perfect house, whose pacings we could hear deep, deep into the evening, a woman who could not rest. She had slender hands with veins that jutted between knuckles hard as walnuts, knuckles she might tap you with, or hit you with, knuckles she would drum against the wall in great distress. She was all heart and fibrillation, my mother, and we pulsed with her, full of her anxiety and intensity, learning through her every move that life was to be lived at operatic pitch, that love came in notes so high they hurt the ears.

Sometimes she looked at me. I, well, I was the middle girl. Compared with my sisters, who always remembered to brush their teeth and put their school clothes out the night before, who ate cooked turnip with not a peep of protest, I was badly behaved. I had ambitions that involved tree houses and turtles. I frustrated her. Sometimes she slapped me, hard, across the cheek. Sometimes she came up to me and rubbed her hand across my burgeoning breasts, a look of tightness—disapproval and desire—on her face. Other times, though, she stroked my hair, which was white-blond and so thin the pink crack of my scalp was always on display. "You," she would say to me during those moments of tenderness. "You are most like me. You have a great drive. That is why we clash."

I think she loved me best, back then.

Now I am a woman with an apple in my hands. I am a woman who has stepped from the opera into silence, a quiet and calm difficult to decode. In making such a move, I am having to learn many new skills, but most of all, it occurs to me, I am having to learn to leave her. This is maybe the hardest part of the pill, the hardest part of health. It is the deepest departure I have ever known.

December 7

My students help. They are Cambodian, and they speak no English. They come from camps on the border of Thailand, where for months, years, they lived with cold and flies. Now they look around them at a new world. Unlike me, they have nightmares, which they tell me about through pictures and weary-looking eyes. I imagine their dreams. They are full of red. A copper gong shudders in a bone-filled field. The Khmer Rouge are coming.

My job is to teach them what the school calls Survival Skills English. It is the first professional position I have ever been able to have. I am teacher and also taught. We must learn the little things. We don't do Shakespeare in this school, but in birth-control pamphlets we decipher the cycles of life and death, the strange sheddings of the womb. We don't read Colette's lines about melons and seas, but, like today, we go to the supermarket and learn from the labels. My students and I consider carrots—C-A-R-R-O-T-S—and compare the nutritional value of soy versus dairy. I learn clocks and teas. There is, for instance, much more in the world than Lipton, a fact I, who have lived my life from plummet to peak, from hospital to hospital, had never quite recognized before. There is Red Zinger and French Vanilla. There is Tension Tamer and Wild Mint.

"Teas," I said to my students today. I held up a box of, you guessed it, Tension Tamer. "Many to choose from in this country." The box pictured a woman lying on the back of a dragon. The dragon, to my delight and dismay, was asleep.

December 9

I am becoming a little bit spiritual, which I'm sure is not a side effect Eli Lilly reports in its literature on Prozac. After work today, I stopped by the bookstore and picked up Merton, a calm Catholic. I read the words of the monk Terrence Kardong. He writes: "We who are permanently camped here see things you don't see at 55 mph. . . . We see white-faced calves basking in the spring sun like lilies of the field. We see a chinook wind in January make rivulets run. We see dust devils and lots of little things. We are grateful."

I could not yet call myself grateful. I am still saying good-bye.

December 10

I have no real furniture. My bed is a foam pad on the floor. My bookshelves are planks and bricks. When I rented this basement apartment, forty-eight hours after being released from my fifth hospitalization a few years back, there were no light fixtures, and I've never bothered to correct that. Bare sockets sprout bare bulbs that cast a stark light and shadow over my space. My kitchen table is an old outdoor grill I found on the street, with a cloth tossed over it. For chairs I have lawn furniture.

Today, walking home from work, I passed by stores on Mass Ave. I've lived in this city my entire life, but I'd always been too ill to bother with these stores. Now I wasn't. In the display windows were old oak rolltop desks, aged pine boxes. Suddenly, my apartment seemed pathetic to me.

I went into a store called One More Tyme, right across from where I live. A little bell giggled above the door when I opened it. A man behind a desk looked up. I saw rows of frosted-glass cups, some with blue and orange flowers dotted along the rims, their necks threaded. When I touched them, they felt oddly warm, as though they had held on to the heat of centuries, the press of palms that had been upon them for years. I picked one up and turned it over and over. "Do you like lamp glass?" the man asked, and then I realized what it was, something to dim and dull the bare bulb, something so small and insignificant, hardly like a hefty bed or a grand armoire, but made with such care, blown slowly, little petals painted in the creases of the glass.

For just a moment, then, I could feel grateful for that.

One hundred and twenty dollars, he told me. A real antique.

Instead, I used my judgment. I did not seize upon the lamp glass, half a week's salary gone. I put it back. I turned away, even while I allowed myself to take it in, inside me, where it still sits. A fluted thing. A flower.

I found a chair on gliders, for fifteen dollars. "Real oak," he told me, "beneath the paint."

I carried it home. My first solid seat. It was old and white, with faint etchwork on its back. I lowered myself into it. I thought of Anne Gold, a patient I'd met in the hospital, on her haunches, her mussed hair down. I said to myself, "Student, this is a chair. C-H-A-I-R. It is what we use in this land. It is a part of our life."

And then I did it. I did what I rarely saw my driven mother do. I sat. Sunlight slanted down on me. The moon rose, a simple silver groove in the sky. I rocked back and forth. There was no noise anywhere, except for the chair, which seemed to chant.

January 4

I took my students to the bank today, so they, well, so we all could learn about money markets, loans, CD's, things I have never known about before. The bank was actually quite fancy, with a thick rug and wainscoted teller counters, perky little faces behind bubbles of plastic. The manager gave us a tour. He took us behind the teller counter and into the bowels of the bank, where we saw the safe and the green bills banded with paper strips. "What is sin?" a voice inside me suddenly asked. I am Jewish by birth and tradition, but in all the years of Hebrew school, I don't remember learning any definition of the term. The God of the Patriarchs, on whom I must have modeled myself, is demanding, driven, and does not reign from a rocking chair.

Now, tonight, I am still thinking about that question. What is sin? I think sin is a failure to grow. Maybe Prozac, by ushering in a kind of contentment, estranges people who were previously religious and striving from growing toward God. In the New Testament there is a story about Jesus coming to visit Mary and Martha one night. Mary sits by Jesus' feet and soaks up his spiritual teachings. Her sister, Martha, on the other hand, cannot stop thinking about dinner and is too busy with the meat loaf or the fish or whatever it was they ate back then to listen. Martha gets frustrated and says, "Mary, come help me," and Jesus replies that Mary is right where she needs to be.

According to conventional Christianity, then, and probably Judaism too, Prozac is a conduit to sin because it makes you more attentive to the tasks, the tiny things, altogether less transcendent. But perhaps, as Merton might say, the truth is in the tiny things, which is why I have for so long used illness to avoid them. Daily tasks—washing, laundering, banking, baking— they force me to my flesh, to the feel of fingers in repetitive movement, to the sloughings and tickings, the burst of a soap bubble, the death of a cell. There is dirt on my dishes, dust on my floor. I am immersed and averse. I struggle for the sky. Stay down. My knees are on the ground. This is where all decay begins, where rot and ripeness live side by side.

January 10

What would a journal be without a weather report? When I was a child I had a little patent-leather diary with its own gold-plated padlock and minuscule key. I started every entry with the weather. "Stormy," I recall writing with a flourish. "Black clouds and wind."

It is dead in the middle of a New England winter

now. Every day the sky is tarnished silver. At night the thermometer plunges to below zero. I can see my own oxygen, which I imagine is the ghost of a former self, taking flight.

What would a diary be without some mention of the landscape? But I cannot see the landscape because of the crusted snow cover. Hill and dale are leveled to white flatness. When new snow falls, the flakes are dry and white and spin over the icy surface. Sometimes, in the mornings, I see ripples and striations in the snow, which remind me of muscle bared from flesh, the essence of energy revealed.

Tonight, either in celebration of the snow or in defiance of it, I decide to take a bath. Baths are not something I normally do; they seem too decadent. What the hell. I put bubbles under the gushing faucet, and they flare into translucence. I lower myself down. Down. It is not, contrary to what the Calgon commercials say, entirely pleasant. I am lowering myself down. Froth comes up to clasp me, closes over me. I stiffen, and then I see her in the shower, shadow of a woman, crescent of breast. All right. I start with the soap, something solid and square, with which I wash my neck. I greet the bubbles cautiously, slowly forgoing the Dial bar for their froth. I scoop some up, smooth over one shoulder, and, while out the bathroom window I see the Big and Little Dipper—in here I suddenly picture planets moving around me in the palm of my hands, at the nape of my neck, stars and suns, one hundred worlds. Here is where I am. This is where I wait. In the bath of small seeds made large by love and imagination. Attention. When I finally stand, streams run off me, and of course, later on, I must scrub the scum from the tub.

February 4

It's been almost a year now since I've composed a short story or a poem, I who always thought of myself as a writer, all tortured and intense. I can just manage this journal. So maybe I'm not a writer anymore. Maybe Prozac has made me into a nun, or a nurse, or worse, a Calgon Lady. Why can't I manage a simple story? Why is my voice—all my voices—so lost to me?

Every morning, before work, I come to the blank page and look at it. It looks like winter. It is February in my mind. I think of the things people have said about the blank page, all the images. Sheet of snow. Anesthetized skin. To those images I add my own: the white of Prozac powder, spread thin.

Basically, good writing is intensity, pitch, sex. Raymond Carver used to say that sometimes, when he was deep into a poem, he would look down to find his hand cupping his balls. I've read that Prozac diminishes the sex drive, so it would stand to reason that it might diminish the by-products of that drive as well, the seduction of language, the cry inside a word. I used to write fast or not at all. Pre-Prozac, I had my days of silence, but they were punctuated by days of rapid flow, my eyes half closed, links of sentences slipping from me. I felt a pressure building, a bodily desire to utter, and then I came, unclasped. Now, in health, there is not the same pressure. I feel a wider range of things. I am broad and open, as though the cyst in my mind has permanently burst and is pleasantly draining.

It occurs to me that during all these years I have written like an adolescent boy has sex. I have come all hot and bothered, bottled in my own hormones, unable, physiologically, to allow foreplay to emerge, a flirtation with a word, a tentative stroke and sculpt to the paragraph, a reaching and receding before consummation. I need to learn to write, as the adolescent has to learn to love, all five bases. There is not just the spasm of orgasm, but mouth and finger and the plateau of uncertainty about the other's body. The body of work before you. Perhaps this journal represents my first attempts to love language differently, to write at lesser levels of arousal. I am not made ecstatic by these entries. Nevertheless, some of the things, like the image of the teas and the thoughts about prayer, I think are pretty good.

I think I could keep them. Or maybe, they will keep me.

February 10

A world I might learn to live in. A world I might learn to love.

February 15

Contemplation, says Merton, can only occur in silence. And contemplation, the ability to experience holiness in the quiet world, is always a gift directly from God. If Merton were alive, I would ask him a few questions. What does it mean, for instance, that my burgeoning contemplative bent does not come directly from God but from Prozac? Might this mean that Prozac is equal to God? This is an awful, awful thought. So turn it around. Primitive cultures often use drugs as a means of accessing their gods. That's better. Maybe Prozac is to the modern world what peyote is to the Indians.

February 23

The brain machine was steel and glass and had an oval lens as wide as a lion's mouth. Thank God I did not have to wear a white hospital robe, or I would have felt like a virgin being fed into the den. I had my regular clothes on, and before I put my head against the sleek and wild lens, the technicians had me drink a sugary fluid that would shoot through my system, branching and curving, entering my skull, leaching through the blood-brain barrier and acting to illuminate the electrical activity in there. Dr. Koskava explained that these sorts of brain scans, apparently new and nifty in the field of neuroscience, work by measuring metabolic activity in the hemispheres. Heat produces pictures. Thus, they heat up your head with sucrose, fructose, get the blood sweet and boiling, and then, properly marinated, you lie down and let the camera shoot.

What I had was called a PET scan, short for positron-emission tomography. Because I'm part of a study about anxiety disorders and medication, the doctors wanted to observe what all that gray paste up there looks like now that it's been dusted with Prozac for so many months. I imagined my brain would look like an old antique globe, a pale bluish gray swathed with soft clouds, distant and dim.

I lay down. A technician turned a computer on, and then the camera on—a whir and growl—*snap snap snap*. Then, out through the slot of a printer came six sheets of paper, each imprinted with an image of my head. The technician showed me. Nothing distant or dim about it. A cerulean blue, a whole hemisphere of orange. Lantern yellow and cool aqua. These are images of my thoughts, the kiss and collide of neurons, the molecular mystery of illness and health. "How does it look?" I asked the technician. "Are these colors normal, or are they signs of, you know—"

"Quite normal," she said. "Everyone's brain is colorful like this. The problem comes when you have too much color concentrated in one area, because that indicates an excess of electrical activity, which could be a sign of a disorder. But not here," she said.

Not now, I thought.

She let me keep a copy of the image. It both comforts and surprises me. At night, hung on my refrigerator, my brain glows in the arc of a headlight. My brain shines in its silence. Something is always happening, always shining, even in a life of small gestures. An act as simple as staring at a house makes your lobes light up birth-blue. Sometimes I touch the lobes. Sometimes, when I am tired, I rest my head against my head.

February 25

    Setting an alarm clock
    The meaning of CD
    Money Market
    FICA

A weekly wage
How to rock

This is a list of all the things I have learned through Prozac. I should also add cooking. My students and I baked corn bread in the school's kitchen the other day, and tonight I decided I could save more of my salary if I prepared at least some things from scratch. Also, I enjoy it, the measuring and sifting, the slow rise.

I was making pumpkin muffins. I knocked over the entire canister of King Arthur's flour, and the floor went white and drifty. Shit. I kicked at the dusty dunes. I tried scooping some up, but because housekeeping is not yet on my What I've Mastered list, I found a little frizzled fly in a mound. I went to sweep it up, but alas, I have yet to buy a broom. Same old story. I had never stopped to consider the need for one before, when I was ill.

Once upon a time, when I was ill—

I knelt before the flour then, and let it fall through my fingers. It was incredibly soft, talc on a grand-mother's cheek. I pressed my hand into it, and then I saw the imprint of my hand like the paw print of a pre-served dinosaur. A memory came to me then. Not a buried memory resurfacing to click the terrible truth into place, but a simple recollection, there, kneeling in the flour. It used to snow and snow. I was six, maybe seven years old. Snow landed on the dried rosebushes, in the slats of our shutters. The yard was enveloped, the trees reverent in their robes. I always went outside in this kind of weather. It seemed to me the angels were dropping stars from the sky. It seemed to me I was called but could not say why, or by whom. Lowering myself into the fresh snow, turning over, opening my arms and legs, swish and sweep, then rolling out to inspect my mold. It was never quite right. A crooked wingspan, a marred head. A compulsion came over me: do it again, and again. All around my yard I tromped, lowering, swishing, sweeping, never to come out right. The next morning I would waken to sun and see the yard covered with my frantic forms, aching attempts toward something I could not name.

And the flour was snow, and the old little compulsion came back to me then. The old crazy little compulsion, as most are. *Make yourself right,* the urge seemed to say. *Make your lines sleek; aim for a symmetry so complete it closes every crack.*

I am not supposed to have these sorts of thoughts on Prozac. Apparently the sick me is still somewhere here. She is hiding behind the branches of my bones. She is peeking out, playful, coy, and pained. Her voice must mix with mine.

I surrendered to it. I surrendered to the compulsion, let the world narrow back to who I once was. Lowering myself into the flour was a reaching back, scary and soothing all at once. I became that girl. The windows of my house are distant ship lights in the sea of snow. My mother moves inside. I am still hers.

When I stood, I saw myself in the flour-white. It was not a perfect image of me but something messy and incomplete. A small voice, a six-year-old, urged *try it again, you must try it again,* in a tone too intense for the task at hand. I considered trying it again, but I am twenty-six now, not six, and I am now on medication whose purpose is to quell these anxious quests, and as I stood there, I felt the urge dim until I could no longer sense its heat.

Prozac is a drug of cool and calm.

But, like every angel I've ever made, I see now that Prozac is imperfect, that through the cracks in its chemistry bits of old illness come through.

Maybe a day of depression here and there. A moment of fierce need.

It recedes, and you are left with space again.

Shush-sh hush-sh, the space says.

You are grateful.

Yes, I am grateful.

I looked at the flour girl, soft, a little sloppy. I leaned

back down, not with compulsion but with curiosity. I would not correct her. I would choose her. I touched the span of her arms, the wide *V* of waking legs. Then I stepped back, observed her from afar. I am observing her even as I write this. She is waving good-bye. She is opening to receive. She is dust and light.

3. Does the patient have a hx of substance abuse? Y/<u>N</u>

4. Primary Substance __N/A__ Secondary Substance __N/A__
Tertiary Substance __N/A__

5. Have there been one or more attempts to cut down or control—

The things we don't say. The things we don't tell. Next to Barbar Jean's there was a store called Skendarian Apothecary. Everything was too expensive for me there, which may have made the items all the more appealing. Crutches with rubber pads, and shelves of cherry medicine. As a child I longed for an injury to deliver me. I longed for a doctor to press his palms against my throat.

When I was very young, I made my own pills from colored sheets of drawing paper. I would tear off little bits and worry them between my thumb and forefinger until a small ball formed, and then I'd swallow my paper pills. I would lie down on the floor of the basement, next to the boiler, and wait for healing to happen.

I loved my paper pills and went so far as to bottle them in empty jam jars. Red pills, green pills, pink pills, pills for my stomach, my head, my ears, my crotch. Sometimes I took several a day, and they moved through me, soothing every inch, lending color to the bits of blandness in my body, even to my scat, which came out like Christmas, all hope and ornament.

Everyone knows. Falling in love is a state of surrender, not necessarily pleasant. Like a depressed person, you let yourself go—your hair, your house, your sleep, all your old beliefs; you just say yes. Yes.

I fell in love one day, only it was not with a person; it was with my pill. Stark naked and delightfully drugged, I sat in that bath of bubbles. I bit into an apple, and I enjoyed the gesture. I enjoyed my white chair on which, over many weeks, I snoozed and rocked, rocked and snoozed, my defenses dwindling down. I started to take more baths, some, even, with petals and scent. Prozac brought me to pumpkin muffins, yellowfin tuna, and plum sauce. Prozac brought me to Harvard, where they accepted me to study—what else?—psychology.

So eventually, yes, my heart was wooed. Like a child introduced to new and fancier foods, I grew, over the first year of my courtship with the pill, to savor the escargot of my life, and then, in some subtle way I cannot quite define, I came to need that nourishment.

Secretly, I started to fear a nuclear war only for the effects it would have on the pharmacies.

Pshaw on those prisses who claim love is not about need.

The thought of going back, oh no.

Riding on the broad back of Prozac, I felt the hospitals were far away. My life became quiet but rich, a fine piece of music by Mozart. What happened is this: I got used to health, and then I got good at it. Ivy League school. Friends and lattes, hey. Hey, it's really OK. Hey. Hey. Don't go away. After about one year of sanguinity, I started some nights to dream that it all did go away, and in the place of light and lather—illness. I woke from these dreams with a bad taste in my mouth. Early one morning, in the half dark of dawn, I woke reaching for Prozac the way you reach for his hand or a hank of his hair. My fist closed in on the bottle, and the connection was complete.

——

It was at this point, about one year into the drug, that I made my declaration. I decided to accept Prozac completely, to declare it an essential and inseparable part of me, my permanent partner in life. To mark this transition, I finally moved out of my basement apartment. I'd been living in that dank place, where there were centipedes on the ceiling, for longer than I could recall. The apartment had black bars over every window and a randy seventy-year-old superintendent with a lung disease.

I moved to a less upscale neighborhood than the Cambridge one where my basement had been, but a neighborhood, nevertheless, with charm, with mansard houses and bright window boxes and clean old folks. This neighborhood had far fewer centipedes and far more dogs, basset hounds with long soft ears, and collies.

I loved my new place. It had a beautiful medicine cabinet, oak with carved rosettes, a medicine cabinet as roomy and handsome as a rich man's den. My Prozac passed its time either in there, or in my mouth.

Other things: the French doors, trimmed with white, the panes of glass sparkling in the light. White walls, floors of oiled oak that reflected a reddish sheen, like an Irish setter's coat. The kitchen, where I hung pots whose copper fannies gleamed continuously, and the living room, where my new Conran's couch sat stuffed and soft against the far wall.

And school, where for the first time I got all good grades and impressed people. I took piles of courses, so many that I would, even though I didn't know it then, get my doctorate in record time. I started an internship at a very famous halfway house for boozers. Now I was really cranking. I loved the boozers, grizzled old Italian men with excellent betting skills. At night they walked me to my car and offered to hire me a hit man should I ever need one. It was with the staff that I felt weird. I had to sign something saying that I would allow them to test me for drugs, if they had any suspicion. At any point they could tell me to pee in a cup, and then I would be revealed. When the boozers talked about things they'd done to scam on urine screens, like drink goldenseal or vinegar, I listened extremely carefully. I crossed one leg casually over the other. The sound of my stockings, a silken swish. Sly. Sly. "So where do you get this goldenseal stuff?" I asked my client Vincent one day. He looked at me and smiled. He had three dead teeth, all black. My mouth felt black and dead too. Vincent leaned forward. He told me where. He stared straight at me, one junkie to another, both of us knowing that crooked kind of love.

—

Falling in love, wonderful as it was, did have its difficulties, even at first. The goldenseal issue. The hiddenness.

The change, first in location, and then in philosophy as well. For instance, some people, when they marry, convert from Judaism to Catholicism, or from Catholicism to Hinduism. Some atheists become born again. I had always been Jewish with a decidedly Cambridge flair. I believed in an ecumenical god. I had a sense of the spiritual that could easily incorporate Christ and witches. I prayed.

My relationship with Prozac, though, caused in me a conversion. At first the pill helped me to appreciate and learn the little things—housework, checkbook balancing, keeping time. And while it did make me more skilled and spiritual in these daily tasks, the drug also drained something larger from my life. I slowly came to see Prozac's point of view, which posits God as a matter of molecules and witchcraft as a neural mishap. In my free time, after work or on Sundays, I went to the library and read whatever I could about my medication's origins.

I was swayed, there in those Harvard libraries or in my psychopharmacologist's office. Maybe I needed to be swayed, to justify this oral intimacy by claiming a shared bevy of beliefs. Eli Lilly, Prozac's progenitors, plus a lot of other independent researchers and commentators, had written a plethora of literature that proclaimed, with the confidence of a trumpet's note, the underlying assumptions. "Behind every crooked thought," I read, "lies a crooked molecule."

I felt a little like I was reading the Psalms, or the Old Testament prophets. The literature of Prozac was an odd combination of poetry and reductionism, cockiness and mist.

Quote. We can conceive of the brain as a kind of computer software, and Prozac is the program that vitiates the virus.

Quote. While correlation does not imply causation, we believe that if a patient is cured by a serotonin-specific chemical, then there are probable anatomical illness correlates in the brain.

Quote. Behind every crooked thought lies a crooked molecule.

Quote. In light of these findings, the patient's past, the story of self, is no longer relevant. We do not need to explain mental illness in the context of history. We can place it, and its cures, firmly in the context of chemicals.

Close quote.

—

After a full twelve months on Prozac, I just couldn't deny these facts any longer. Prozac is, after all, an especially gifted proselytizer. I had been ill for years and years, and I had tried deep breathing, talking, vitamins, and jogging. I had spent embarrassingly large chunks of time in a relatively nice nut house, where the kitchen walls were yellow and Minnie Cleave, the retarded woman, played the same song on the piano all day. Three blind mice. See how they run. Three blind mice. See how they—

See. I saw. We were software and hardware, wires in the heart. Silicon chips gave a gleam to our eyes. We had necks of steel and tongues of zinc. Our stories were a series of electrical impulses, maybe difficult to decode but oh so easy to deconstruct.

—

Into my life at this time, at this sweet and empty pinnacle, came a real man, and because Prozac is an especially vital and polygamous partner, loving many men and women the whole world over, I started something with this real man too. Here was Bennett, with a blond beard and a lovely mouth. His lashes were so pale, especially when the sun shone on them, and his eyes were bits of an Alaskan sky, a cool white-blue. It should come as no surprise that my Bennett was a chemist, that he passed his time among swan-throated glassware and Pyrex pipets, that in the back pocket of his polyester khakis he always kept a copy of the atomic chart, which he liked to read to me instead of romantic poetry. He never directly serenaded my skin, although I wished he would. I wished he would one day just lapse into sense-less stanzas, into a jungle of useless beauty, and pro-claim something smutty and gorgeous like "When I fuck you it's sliding into a satin slipper, only softer and honey to taste."

That was not Bennett's way, a factless gush. How-ever, he, like Prozac, did tell me many a splendid tale. Bennett told me our whole world is comprised of only six basic properties—hydrogen, oxygen, nitrogen, sul-fur, carbon, phosphorous. And truly there is a kind of primitive poetry to that statement, something rhythmic and essential.

And then one day I was sitting on my couch. I had just sucked down my second dose. Bennett came to my door, a rose in hand. The flower was carnal red, with intricate navel folds. "For you," he said, but when I tried to take it, he pulled it away. "My finest feat," he said. "A real chemical wonder."

A bowl from the kitchen, liquid nitrogen in a bottle hidden in his bag. He emptied the bottle into the bowl. "The coldest chemical on earth," my scientist an-nounced, or something like that. Before I even touched the ruby rose, he dipped it in the liquid nitrogen and pulled back out a frozen flower, a glassed-in growth, color and form perfectly preserved.

"Wow," I said. I meant it.

"We're not through," he said. "I love you. We will never be through."

And with that he bowed, smiled, and hurled my rose at the wall, whereupon, after a perfect click of contact, it broke into hundreds of icy beads.

Hydrogen, nitrogen, oxygen.

So damn easy to deconstruct.

And yet the beads were beautiful, flakes of snow, scarlet hail.

Even great love can be lonely.

—

Understand, I had been sick my whole life. I had been *hobbled,* and now I wasn't, and so, in the midst of my affairs with my medicine and my boyfriend, I decided to take a trip. Mental illness has many qualities, foremost among them its smallness and ridiculous repetition. I was a very boring madwoman. Almost all I could discuss was the number of times I'd tapped on the stove, the number of calories I had consumed, or how blah I felt. I had rarely left Boston because of fear, the fancy name for which is agoraphobia. Of all the things to be scared of, I was scared of space, and that's such a shame, because space is everywhere, and therefore so is fear.

Somewhere in the world, I knew, there were golden cupolas. I knew there were oceans that looked like moving marble. I knew that on ponds in Europe swans drifted beneath a pink sky.

Now, a well woman, I wanted at least some part of it. Maybe I could go to Africa, where I would live in a mud hut and ululate. Or England, to the dreary and gorgeous moors.

I finally decided on Kentucky, because that's where I got the grant to do the thesis research that would support my trip. I went in the summer—school break, internship over—which is a terrible time to visit Kentucky, the temperatures hitting one hundred degrees day in, day out, all the chickens miserable.

What did I know?

What did my doctor know? He was Eastern European, for God's sake, and certainly couldn't warn me about the weather in the American South.

Still, he might have warned me about some other things.

"A great idea," he said. He wrote me a prescription.

I couldn't take Bennett with me, but of course I could take Prozac. One lover was better than none. Koskava's prescription covered three months, 278 pills, so many capsules they filled four fat amber vats, vats of such shameless girth they would not fit into any of my knapsack's pocket compartments. I considered the pos-sibility that I would have to get my own separate luggage set just for my meds. That seemed like a shame, trudging off into the yonder with such an obvious sign of capitulation, of weakness, like a lady taking a hair dryer with her into the jungle. At last I came upon a solution. I hid the little loves in my mess kit, filling my capacious canteen with my pills, every last one of them, *plink kerplink,* as they hit the hollow sides, then silence as the swarm filled, full, my space.

—

I, who had barely been out of Boston before.

—

I drove, all confidence and cheer. I went smack across the country, powered by the passion of Prozac.

I stopped to see the salt mines in Pennsylvania. They were tall and slender brides beneath the blue parasol of sky.

In Ohio I visited the Museum of Natural History. I saw dead reptiles and pickled ants. I read plaques that explained the chemical etiology of the cricket's song, the mosquito's fondness for blood. I had a mini anxiety attack in that museum. I was surrounded by roaches and rats and spiders, and I felt like I fit right in. What, really, is the difference between a human being and a bug? Two species, separated only by an accident in evolution, a mere bulge in the brain, but otherwise the same. Both, all, everything, a maze of crisscrossing wires, neural blips. It's hard to have solid self-esteem with a view like that. Prozac's view, and now mine, that history is meaningless, stories no more than convenient construction. That the person, a mere concoction of chemicals, is programmed from birth.

Pure beast.

—

When I was a child, my family had a little lapdog, a very froufrou canine with big hair. My mother insisted it wear bows and knitted sweaters and be groomed weekly. One day I decided to give the dog a pedicure. I flipped it on its back and held its paw up to my desk lamp, where I filed and then proceeded to paint. I did each long nail a Revlon red. I did not achieve the desired effect, which was to make the animal only more elegant, and thus please my impossible mother. Instead, when I was done, our little dog looked wild, looked wolf, like he had been hunting and had come upon a big kill.

—

Despite the hunting and moonshine and murders in Kentucky, it was a state, I soon discovered, with a lot of God in it. There were churches everywhere. The family I stayed with had a Jesus on every wall. On the wall right across from my bed there was a large plastic Jesus, which I took some time to study. He was crucified, of course, with nails in all the tender places. He was very thin, possibly anorexic, and his skin was white and pink. A tiny and dirty-looking loincloth covered his crotch. Sometimes I would sneak and touch him, which gave me the shivers. I could feel the molded muscle, the prominence of ribs. His hair was hardened honey, his lashes lacquered with grief. I could touch the pupils of his eyes—dabs of blue—and feel how the blood welled forever from his wounds. I could sense the tension in his neck, and I soon discovered that I could slide the tip of my finger into his pain-parted mouth. One night, when I was unable to sleep and it was very late, I did something I still don't really understand. I fed Jesus some Prozac. I eased a pill in between his lips, where, with some prodding, it fit. I stepped back to see. The tip of the Prozac protruded from his mouth, a little green berry, a bubble, we would fly. I observed him in this pose for a long time. Looking back on it now, I think this is when I started, again, to lose my mind. Finally I fell asleep, and in the morning when I woke up, Jesus, a man wedded to his suffering, looked a little angry, and the Prozac pill was gone.

—

This is really what I mean to say. The Prozac pill was gone. Gone! First I had a mini anxiety attack in the bug museum, and then I started having trouble sleeping, and then, one morning, two weeks into my Kentucky trip, I woke up a madwoman again. The Prozac had simply stopped working. That's impossible. No, it's not. I started to tap and touch things and to have to count until my mind clenched closed. *Where are you, Prozac? Come home, come home. Back to my body again.* This, I now know, is what the boozers must feel when they drop a full bottle and it breaks against the ground. Or what women must feel when their husbands leave for bagels on a Sunday morning and later drop a line from Katmandu. When you fall so deeply in love, when you have, with great consideration, tied the slow satin knot, you don't expect to be betrayed. But then you are.

—

And of all the places to crack up, Kentucky. Crack-ups are always terrible, but this one was so sudden, and so complete. It was as though Prozac had never existed. My mental illness came rushing back in. As fast as Prozac had once, like a sexy firefighter, doused the flames of pain, the flames now flared back up, angrier than ever, and my potent pill could do nothing to quell the conflagration. How horrible. I was counting, checking, tapping, walking backward, and getting stuck in doorways. Not only was it devastating—it was also very humiliating.

—

"She is odd," I heard Great-Aunt Mary whisper to Kat, the mother of the family who had kindly agreed to house me.

"May I use your phone?" I squeaked to Kat. From far across the country, I heard the ringing in the doctor's office, but he didn't pick up. He was on vacation.

"Come to church with us," Kat said. "We can see you're ill, suffering from some city sickness." And then she hesitantly reached out, smoothed back my sweaty bangs. I am still in touch with Kat today, years later, and she is a woman of resonant kindness.

I did go to church with them, with Kat and her husband, Lonny, and Great-Aunt Mary, and the children, Bridget and Kim. Here, they told me, I would be healed. And truly the church was beautiful, a tiny stone structure high up on a hill. It was Sunday, and very quiet, and fog draped delicately over everything, and the church windows glowed like piles of wet candy.

And inside everybody bowed their heads, and the sun, when it finally came through the stained glass, was the color of taffy and rose. And everyone stood, and there was the sweet meaty music of gospel, and a few loose folks writhing on the floor and crying for joy, and Kat led me to the preacher, who painted a cross of oil on my forehead and told God to get a move on and make me well right here. Right here! Right now.

"I'm well," I said, blinking my eyes.

"She's well!" the preacher shouted in jubilant tones. The whole church went into overdrive, sounded like a football stadium, everyone clapping and hailing and praising the Lord and rolling around between the pews.

I felt a little guilty about that, because in truth I didn't feel any better at all, but I thought it would be polite to say I did. I mean, when you go to someone's house for dinner you say the food is good no matter what. I figured the same manners applied to visiting a church, only instead of praising the food you praised the efficacy of the prayers, and now I had made a mistake. They practically wanted to crown me for letting the Lord in, and so quickly at that.

Oh, it was nothing, I said, smiling. I was bothered by the feeling of oil on my forehead. I swore it was dripping. I kept wanting to count the drips.

And the whole way home, riding with the family in the car, I kept wishing I had been made well. I kept wishing I could believe in that kind of remedy, the touch of an old-fashioned God lighting up a life. Prozac had betrayed me, the bastard, but not before its belief system had leached to the very root of me, the belief that, when all is said and done, we are ultimately beast, that we are beyond the saving grace of story, that only chemicals can cause hurt, and thus, only chemicals can cure.

——

It took Kat and Lonny and Great-Aunt Mary only a few hours to see that I was, indeed, not well. As soon as they observed me walking backward again, they knew. "The Lord works in mysterious ways," I said. "If He has entered my life once, maybe He will do so again."

I wasn't picturing the Lord when I said that. I was, of course, picturing Prozac.

When the Prozac Doctor finally decided to get back from vacation, two weeks had passed and I was sick as a dog, my whole mind warped. Really, I should have returned to Boston, but I was too proud. He picked up the phone.

"What is this stuff?" I said. "What is this stuff you gave me? It was working perfectly, and now it's not. I've built up a tolerance to it. This stuff is like heroin. What's going on here?"

"Prozac is not like heroin," the doctor said, a little defensively, I might add.

"Well, then, what happened? I'm taking my doses every day, and I might as well be swallowing a sugar pill. Explain it to me. Explain it to me," I said, and my voice was frantic.

So he did. He told me how the medical community was just discovering this problem in long-term Prozac users. "It's called Prozac poop-out," he said.

"Prozac poop-out," I said. "You've got to be kidding me." I was taking a drug with a prostate problem, a drug with sexual dysfunction, a goddamn impotent little Prozac penis . . .

"Why didn't you warn me?" I said. "You have no idea"—I started to cry—"no idea how shocking this is. I have come . . ." I said, and I gripped the receiver hard. "I mean, I had come to really love, I mean, really depend on this stuff, for my functioning."

"It's OK," the doctor said. "We can always up your dose. Take eighty milligrams instead of sixty. Let's see what happens."

"You tell me," I said, "what happens when we have the little poop-out problem at eighty milligrams. Then what do we do? Keep upping my dose till I die?"

He paused, like he might actually be considering that possibility.

"Let's see what happens at eighty," he said, and then he hung up.

I wasn't going to take the eighty, though, and get all better, only to fall flat on my face again. The point wasn't eighty milligrams. The point was getting my old relationship with the pill back. And I didn't see how that would happen, now that I had been betrayed. Sad to say, on top of my obsessive illness I also became a Woman Who Loves Too Much. I yearned and pined in the privacy of my Appalachian bedroom. I lifted an amber pill bottle and rolled it against my cheek. A catch in my heart, a click in my throat. I took a pill and held it between thumb and forefinger. I went so low as to lick it. Other times I imagined it hatching like an egg and from between the split shells a handsome man stepping out, a lawyer or a doctor with green eyes and a B.A. from Princeton. A gourmet cook in his spare time, he would make me golden polenta and tomato with basil. Large scarlet wheels of ripeness sprinkled with papery green. Something steams. He hands me a glass of deep red wine, and I am redeemed.

—

Maybe I was tired of groveling. Or maybe, more likely, the rage at the doctor, the rage at the illness, the rage at the two-timing pill, rose up and ran over. Because there was a time, at the very end of my Kentucky trip, when things shifted. I had gotten very little research done, and I didn't know how I would explain that to my funders. I had exhausted myself with counting and checking and had finally fallen into a dreamless sleep. I dimly heard the sound of a storm moving over the region, the tin-top clatter of hail on the roof, and I dimly sensed the sudden sweep of clearing that happens in Kentucky, clouds yanked like rags from a washline, the sudden sparkle of blue. I sensed it, and slept through it, and when I woke it was late afternoon and the sky was the color of pearl.

I was in no mood for pearl. I was in no mood for prettiness. I woke up suddenly, a howl in my mouth, my hands clenched. I was raging and roaring to go. I was in a genuine Gloria Gaynor mood, and in my mind I was belting out, "Go on now/Go walk out the door/ Just turn around now/'Cause you're not welcome anymore."

And then I was outside, walking, pushing past the need to count before every blessed step. I was sick of being sick. I was sick of being betrayed. I was sick of being so thoroughly and pathetically passive, my mouth always hanging open like a ripped pocket. No.

There were red rags tied around sticks marking the path I was on. They were there to scare the skunks from the harvest. I just dared a skunk to approach me. I would twist its head off.

And I was walking, thinking these angry thoughts (ahh, anger, I can hear some feminists say. The antidote to illness. Perhaps it's true), and from across the field I saw a funnel form, black and spinning, almost wooly.

Good. A tornado. I'd punch it out. No problem. I had lost my mind.

I had come to the very end, which is also the beginning.

I held my ground as this bit of black weather approached me. Later on, I would learn this was not a real tornado I'd prepared myself to fight but something far less spectacular, a devil duster, supposedly harmless; but to me it was, and always will be, a bona fide twister.

It came prancing across the field like a wicked girl, snatching up daisies and grass, and as it came closer I felt wind and grit flail my face, and I anchored myself back, hard on my heels, and put up my very best dukes as I watched the vegetation get ripped up by its roots. And then it stopped, right in front of me, still spinning but not moving forward anymore; a windy, whooshing spirit, it bowed, cavorted, beckoned me to come inside. My mind got very quiet. The funnel was a world, inside it dust and rocks and pollen whipped up into a primitive stew. The funnel slapped at the red rags tied to the sticks, and then it picked those up too; separate swatches spun faster and faster until at last they blended together, a perfectly fused flower, Bennett's broken rose returned to me whole, here, mine. Me. I lifted.

—

Yes. In the very end, which is also the very beginning, I said yes to that.

—

And then the funnel moved off.

—

All around me it was quiet, and some branches were down, and a loosened fence slat went *rat tat tat*.

—

Doors in me had opened. Elegance had entered.

—

I sat on a stump in the field. I could feel the compulsions coming back into my brain, the little itches and urges that, by sheer accretion, finally decimate. I waited for them to take me over, but I also said, *Now, wait a minute*. I also noticed how I could notice the stump I sat on, its reddish rings and the termite snacking at its base. I thought the bug was a termite because it seemed to be eating the wood, but it turned out to be a beetle, and two wings of chitin parted to reveal a black bodice beneath, the frilly and delicate torso of an insect that finally moved into flight.

—

I noticed I could notice, as though even in the depth of illness, there was a camera in my brain, clicking, recording, preserving, and presenting the world to me.

That thing with the devil duster had been, for sure, a genuine moment. I should have a real camera. I saw perfectly the picture I would take. It would be a picture not actually of the devil duster, but of a girl watching the devil duster, her eyes cleared, her tattered mind momentarily stilled, her skin in a silver net of wonder.

The direct translation of Freud's term *superego* is "over I." Maybe what Freud really meant is not a punishing voice but the bits of self that manage to rise above the chemicals of illness, the chemicals of cure, and even for a moment take in the world from its own ethereal ledge.

Yes?

—

The purple silk of a plum. Sun on a green plate. Over the next few days, even in the thicket of obsessions, these genuine moments occurred—perhaps they always had but I had never noticed them or given them their value—split-second snappings of the shutter, the *click* of freedom. Then closed.

I wondered if I could make these snippets enough for me. It was, I saw, a question of value, of economics, and I could dub the product pricey or poor. Let's not get sentimental. Making a series of shutter-cut, single moments enough to live by in an existence otherwise torn by illness is pretty meager fare. But I was stubborn and mad, and ever since I learned how to play Capture the Flag as a kid, I have hated to lose. Could I maybe learn to live there, in the interstices of illness, in the slivers between synapses, which no one has yet been able to measure? Might that be the free space I could choose to cultivate?

Choose. That word. That thing separating humans from other life-forms, from beetles, bees, and pigs. Choice was its own sort of funnel with a force. It had a shape in my mouth. So long as I could choose anything at all, I was more than my chemicals, more than my cure.

I would do it not because that's what I wanted—I wanted so much more!—but because the knowledge of freedom, the freedom to pick my moments of sustenance, the freedom that, for your information, Eli Lilly, no beast has, gave me at least some of my dignity back.

So there.

—

This was no triumph. Put away that trumpet. I felt like hell, which is a place only people can go.

—

One week after the devil duster, I decided to follow the doctor's suggestion and up my dose to eighty. That's four pills daily, the Big Mac of medicine, and it made me nauseous. I had to take it with two-percent milk.

The Dairy Council would be happy to know that drugs made of me a milk drinker, so even if I was killing myself on the one hand with high doses of Prozac, I would at least die with strong, white bones.

—

I didn't die. I am still here. I could up my dose precisely because I learned, in that field in Kentucky, that I didn't absolutely need to, that if the higher dose betrayed me, I had found something in myself to fall back on. The higher dose did help, though. Some of the *one two three; tap tap tap, step on the crack or break your mother's back* receded, but Prozac never again made me as well as it once had. The poop-out problem has remained but not completely. Why, in all the hoopla about this wonder drug, doesn't anyone mention the poop-out, which a lot of long-term Prozac users experience? I think it's an essential part of the story, really. I still need my stories. And the ending is this. Prozac is not my lover any longer but over the very long haul has become a close friend, a slightly anemic, well-meaning buddy whose presence can considerably ease pain but cannot erase it.

And, really, the relationship is better that way— even though I mourn the passing of my passion— because the great break-up has forced me into my own muscles.

I lift weights at the gym now.

I am superb on the StairMaster.

Yesterday I had a very bad afternoon, and then I noticed a bit of beauty.

"Stop checking the stove for a moment," Bennett said to me yesterday, when it was bad, "and come watch my *Datura ferox* bloom."

Sometimes, at night, when I cannot go to sleep because I must inspect the battery in every smoke detector, Bennett comes out into the hall, rubbing one eye with his fist, and looks at me up there, on the ladder. "Come down here," he says.

Now that Prozac in its old incarnation is gone, I am left open for the love of a living being.

I wish I was 100 percent in my mind.

On a good day I am 70 percent. On a bad day, the repetitions and the grief cannot be counted.

"Come down from there," my Bennett says. I come down.

"You're obsessing," he says. "A blip in the serotonin system." But unlike Prozac, he can speak outside of this language. He can speak with his hands. He comforts me. He takes me to him, and in his touch I feel how I am human.

6. Last grade patient completed ___College___

7. Describe vocational and occupational functioning, including jobs held in past 5 years.

Little voc. history to speak of. Patient graduated from college with spotty academic rec. Dropped out of grad. creative writing school aft. one sem. Since then, has held a variety of mostly menial jobs—usually fired. Sometimes quit. Patient's occupational abilities compromised by psychopathology, both her obsessive style and the identity diffusion typical of a personality—

True, I have many voices. I speak like a let-down lover, a diarist, a social critic, straight sass. I fear I am everything, which of course amounts to being nothing.

Did I tell you about our house? Did I tell you about its gabled roof, its six chimneys, its lawn where on summer nights I sometimes ran, finding frogs between blades of grass? I know I told you of our panic buttons, our alarm. The system was intricate and pricey and technologically very advanced for the 1970s. The panic buttons you had to push—digitally dependent things—but the rest of the system worked by motion detectors and needed only a simple flick of the wrist, a single stride, to set it off. Once my mother activated the system, which she did every night after the late news, we were not allowed to leave our beds without calling first. Three A.M. Four A.M. Mom. Mom. I need the bathroom. And she would rise and snuff the sensors for as long as our salty streams lasted.

One night a bat flew into our house, and in the darkness of a hot July, the flying mammal set off the bells. Yes, the sight was magnificent, frantic flight giving way to ever-increasing symphonies of sound, the bat's body itself lifted on the siren's pulse, its sheer reddish wings stretched like nylon over piping of bone.

My secret desire was to be so detected, to soar on pure sound. After the bat, I decided to try it. I woke very late. I walked down the long hall, full of sprawling shadows and the sound of sleepers turning in their beds. I stood in front of the upstairs sensor, with its green light blinking rhythmically in the night. I did a jumping jack. Nothing happened.

I waved my arms and tossed my head. Still silence. I stood there for a long time, trying to give my movements meaning. I tried a sexy sashay, a stick-'em-up pose, and finally, my very best, a beautifully crafted cartwheel. In the quiet.

Even before I took Prozac, you see, way back in a past that might not even matter, this question of identity existed. I stood in front of an alarm so finely calibrated it could catch the fall of a leaf, a shadow's dart. But not me. Which is why, I think, I started to narrate myself as she—she—the most distant and impenetrable of the persons. She walks. She talks. But, apparently, her motion is motionless, her matter a mirage. She has synthetic skin, no smell. You can try to take her in, but she evades you, lover. She is slippery. She cannot be sensed.

THE THIRD PERSON

One morning he wakes up and says, "Okay. I want to marry you."

"You don't really know me," she says. "I could be a killer."

"Friend or foe," he says, "you're the woman I love."

"I could be a pedophile."

"We could poke some holes in your diaphragm," he says, "and have us some pups."

"They would be pups pickled in Prozac," she says. "Pups with bad brains."

"You'll go off the stuff," he says, "for the nine months it takes."

"Ten months actually," she says, and looks up at the ceiling, where lately there have been leaks, yellowish water staining the clean stretch of white that just last year she had so perfectly painted.

"I don't think I could," she says softly. "Go off the Prozac."

So many things might happen if she did. She might descend again. She might find herself back there. He is so cavalier. He has never known her without her meds, and the stories she's told him about those times do not suffice. She imagines it happening now, in her current life. A kind man, he would come to visit her. She sees him see her in the hospital corridor, next to a nurse. Her hair is ratty, the way, long before she met him, it sometimes used to be. Her lips are dry but bloated from the bulimia, maybe, or from all the drugs that did not work. And he is holding up his hands, going "Whoa, whoa, I didn't know," or saying "OK, OK," as he backs away, and then she sees herself in a small, square room, sun the color of clarified butter flowing in through a single window, flowing into a space very clean, and much too quiet.

Killer, not. Pedophile, not, but something other than what he observes this morning, what he has observed for the time they've been together. Her surface is synthetic. On Prozac she has had a series of steady successes, a seemingly smooth and swift ascension from

master's degree to doctoral degree, from alcohol counselor to psychologist. It is a lie.

She reaches over, puts a hand up to his eyes, and
remembers a long time ago, a girl, and how the eye
doctor parted the pink lips of her lids and squirted
some stuff into her pupils so for a moment the whole
world was filled with fog and burning. "Don't be blind,"
she says to him. "A man as smart as you."

"Don't be condescending," he says. "I can see just
fine. So you have a history." He says *history* like he's
hissing. "So you've had some hard times. So you do
better on a drug. The whole world does better on
drugs. Caffeine. Nicotine. Whiskey. Wine."

—

He himself feels comfortable with drugs. He is like
that, hippie-ish, with long tawny hair pulled back in a
ponytail. His father is famous for his groundbreaking
work on the politics of the drug war and the general
harmlessness of heroin. He adores his father in a way
she finds a little, well, blind. He and his father have
dropped acid together, which she does not approve of.
Some nights she comes home and the house smells
sweet and she finds scraps of charred rolling paper on
the floor, which she unrolls, like a scroll, like a ban-
dage, stray flakes falling out.

—

Once her arms were bandaged. Now they are almost perfect. However, if you look very closely you will see a mesh of small scars all up and down, forearm, shoulder, wrist. Her suicide attempts were never very impressive, but the cutting she did with passion and intention. The scars, of which she is now so self-conscious, attest to that, and therefore, she does not like to tan. Scar tissue resists the sun. While the rest of the flesh goes golden, it stays white. It will not be blended. A well-meaning friend once suggested she have cosmetic surgery to erase the marks. The idea upset her. She was surprised that it upset her. But listen. Every day she takes pills whose purpose is to hide her history. She needs some sign, some inscription. Even if no one can see it, the truth is there. Her writing is on the wall.

—

In many ways, they are a fine match. They are cerebral sorts and have long conversations about the history of this and that well into the night. Their sex life can be difficult—a side effect of Prozac—and this at times is a problem, but he accepts it. He also accepts her bouts of obsessive behavior, her spasms of depression—the lingering remnants of illness—and she accepts his sloppiness, and the monster movies he insists on watching.

That she does not feel known, that all her accomplishments do not feel hers, feel fraudulent, well, isn't that the case for a lot of people? Don't many yearn for absolute intimacy and fear deep entry is impossible? Imposter, imposter, a voice mocks. On the cover of Peter Kramer's famous book about Prozac there is a picture of a person pulling off a mask, a flame-green world around him, his limber body leaping into the light.

She would like to redo that cover. If she had carte blanche, she would design a cover of a book about Prozac picturing an old, Rapunzel-style tower. The sky would be a pastel blue. There might be a lizard or two. A cover of holograms, turn it this way and people appear, women, all of them, in velvet evening gowns, in Joan and David shoes, dancing, drinking tea, black stockings pulled over their skulls.

—

It may be coincidence, or it may be a subconscious effort to shed the stocking; one day they find themselves going back. They have just seen a movie in a far suburb, and on the way home she says, "No. Turn right."

"That won't take us to the highway."

"Turn right," she says. "I want to show you something." Her voice is insistent, imploring. She has realized that with a few out-of-the-way twists and turns she can

138 · Lauren Slater

take him back to the neighborhood where she grew up. At fourteen she was fostered out, and she doesn't see her parents much, but she still, sometimes, ventures back here, to the old neighborhood, and when she does she is usually alone. Sometimes she has parked her car, even, and walked the old streets, and she has found how she recalls them, their shortcuts and culverts, their hidden niches, how stubborn memory is, how, like a series of scars, it marks the brain, imprinting it with passages of the past.

He turns right, and then they are driving down small suburban streets, passing a store called Barbar Jean's, which is, remarkably, still in business, and she says, "I used to buy my candy there."

"What are we doing?" he says. "Where are we going?"

They pass a tennis court with a single spotlight shining down on it and two people on either side of the net, dressed in simple whites, the yellow ball floating like a planet between them.

"Let's go to the house where I grew up," she says. "I want to show you."

This is two months after the A.M. marriage proposal, the talk of children, and the conversation has hung between them since then, a series of things unanswered.

They are on her street now, Walnut. Ahead of them

the house looms, massive, its six chimneys rearing up into a darkening sky, its Georgian pillars with a creamy sheen in the night. No one has lived here for years and years. Her younger sister tells her that after their family broke apart, a wealthy Moroccan couple bought the house but for some unfathomable reason never moved in. The windows are boarded up now, but the gardens have been mysteriously groomed, plump roses draping over marble figurines.

"Wow," he says, as he eases the car up the gravel slope, headlights illuminating the front door with its knocker shaped like a lady's hand. "Wow," he says again. "This place is really something."

"Let's stop," she says. There is a catch in her voice, the tang of salt in her throat. "Let's get out and walk around."

Their car doors click open and closed in the dusk, a sound so precise and defined it is almost lovely. "You're sure we're allowed?" he says. "I mean, aren't we trespassing?"

"No one lives here anymore," she says.

They stand together at the crest of the driveway. Above them two huge elms spread in green clouds. In the distance, a faint but persistent burbling. "What the hell is that?" he says, his voice taut.

She knows just what it is and leads him to it, the

stone fountain in the palladium, covered now with moss, the murky water dotted with dead frogs.

"This is so fucked up," he says. He stared at her. *You say you want to have children with me,* she thinks. She wants him to see through. She wants to be transparent so he may observe the shape of her bones, her uterus, the veins, where liquid rushes, carrying her helixed genes, her hemoglobin, her history of red and tilted things.

She smiles at him, a wobbly smile. She takes his hand. She loves him. She is suddenly aware of loving him profoundly as they stand there together, because he is a brave and kind man, because he has humor and quirkiness, because his hair is tawny and his breath has the scent of fennel.

He looks back at her. His hand stays slack in hers, and she feels frightened by that, but also she is edging toward relief, for he may, at last, be seeing her behind her stocking.

They walk. The ground is spongy. A rotting post rises out of the ground. "This," she says, "is where I used to tie my rabbit so she could graze." And then her rabbit is there, white, with garnet eyes glowing; she is sleeping, she is dreaming, her whole head open to the air.

Scared. And at the same time, the human urge to be opened and observed urges her on. "There," she says, in a low voice as they round a corner on the south side. "Look up there. My bedroom window."

"I see," he says.

"When I was ten," she says, "I stopped being able to leave my bedroom," and she thinks back to that time, the fear that took over, and it could have been then the illness started, or it could have been before, when she woke one night and heard voices in the wires in the walls, or it could have been—the worst of all— something she was born with, a simple physiological fact pressed into her genes. She knows that's the fash- ionable explanation these days, and it's way too simple, of that she's sure, but her mother . . . just screaming and screaming in the center of the kitchen, her father so sad. Once, in the hospital, a social worker drew her a geneagram, a tree with every family member's name and diagnosis boxed in its branches, and the tree went on and on, out and out in flaring illness, and she laughed and said, "The simplest cure might be to just cut it down."

"And there," she says now, pointing.

He follows her finger to the master-bedroom window.

"That's where they slept," she says, "and where she had us watch the movies—"

"Yes, the movies," he says softly, "about the camps."

And then he stops. He has heard every story. He under-stands the violence, but for the first time, there with him now, she can see the knowledge's impact, see how he is feeling the taproots of her time.

"And here," she says, coming to another corner. "Behind that window over there was our kitchen."

"She was an excellent cook, your mother was," he says. "You've told me about her baked Alaska."

"Absolutely," she says. "And her soufflés."

"The flourless chocolate cake."

"Yes," she says. "My mother was talented. She was an artist, really."

"But that was also the kitchen," he says, and pauses, "where she forced you to swallow—"

"Yes," she says, and then she can feel, again, the detergent's stinging in her throat, and she is surprised by how well he has heard her, how he can recall the pre-cise geography of her family's rage.

They pass the old servants' quarters at the back of the house and then stop in the side yard, by the oak tree where she and her brother once labored for weeks to build a tree house. The actual tree house itself is gone, but the wooden rungs, nailed to the trunk, have remained, still surprisingly sturdy, and she starts to climb them. "Don't do that," he says, grabbing her ankle, "those rungs could fall any minute." She keeps going anyway. She keeps climbing. She pulls herself into the crotch of the oak, and then, reaching up with her arms, hoists herself higher, and higher still, slithering her body between the dense leaves, damp on her skin, the sky coming closer, and then she imagines she is climbing the geneagram tree, the one that social worker drew for her, pushing aside the bones of her progenitors, the barky, scaly skin, the narrow knothole of a bitter mouth; there is sadness here. There is regret to the left. She is climbing out of it. Or deeper into it, surrounded by the hearts of leaves, the hearts of humans. And then, when she can climb no farther, when she reaches nearly to the top, she stops and fits herself to the shape of the branches she rests on, so she becomes the body of the tree, a part of the wood's weave, and in the next second something separate from it, a being that has learned to change direction and seek its own star of light.

—

"What are you, crazy?" he says when they are back in the car. "You could've broken your neck."

"I used to climb all the time when I was a kid," she says.

"Kids are crazy," he says.

"I could be crazy," she says. "I've tried to warn you about that."

A little later they pull into their own driveway and get out. It is completely dark now. A neighborhood dog is barking, short staccato sounds, sounds that have been severed with a knife. Also, there is blood on her arm. Inside the house, in the privacy of the bathroom, she inspects this scarlet surprise, each scrape the size and shape of those she used to make on herself. It must have happened on a branch.

When she comes out of the bathroom, he is lying in bed, reading a book. "What were you doing in there, so long?" he asks.

"I cut myself," she says, and holds out her arm to him, as she has held it out to psychiatrists and social workers and mental-health aides on hospital floors so many times. Would he think the visit had caused her to relapse? She holds her arm out to him, a lie, a truth, both of these things.

"From the tree," he says. "It happened on the tree." He looks at her not with suspicion, but with confidence and understanding, a look that says he knows what she is staging here. "You hurt yourself on the tree," he repeats, "while you were climbing it," and then he pulls her close, studies the scrapes on her skin. His name is Bennett, and he is a find. She, of course, is me, which we knew all along, our hiding places, our masks, even when chemically constructed, so much more permeable, so far less mysterious, than ever we think.

And then he pulls me even closer to him, and for the first time he studies the other scars as well, the raised white wisps of tissue that will not be blended, will not be bronzed. "These are the old marks," he says with great deliberateness, "from another time, and I know they are there, Lauren, really I do."

Lauren. She. Me. So many pieces. Really, it is a way of being rich. The pieces could be history to hand to a child.

And then he is not talking anymore; he is touching those places, tracing the old, closed cuts with his fingers, following their undulations, reading them with his eyes shut, like a blind man absorbing braille, touch giving way to tales—once upon a time—he reads it all. He touches it all, who I—she—me—was before Prozac, who we all might still somehow be, and his fingers, slow, soothing strokes, tell me he can care for me beyond the pill. Before the pill. Ratty, bloated, baby, cries; all the people who we are, who we may have, first, second, and third.

had been dosing myself for five years when I saw the article. A handful of British women, all of them on Prozac, were reporting an odd side effect. Whenever they sneezed now, they had an orgasm. This event remains unexplained and has gone down as one of the grand mysteries of the pill—the nose, serotonin, and the genitals conversing in a Morse code scientists cannot crack. Is this phenomenon British-specific, something about those proper Anglicans swallowing their sneezes for years and now, drugged and disinhibited, taking exquisite pleasure in their proboscis? Or is, indeed, the side effect international, but only the Brits have had the courage to confess? For a long while after I read that story I pictured it, little London ladies with sinusitis taking hankies—oh, those hankies, cut from the cloth of satin, silk, and frills—and pressing them to their swollen noses, the *ahh* before the *choo* drawn out in demure ecstasy, for the pollen in the air was thick and floating, tiny orange spheres, the shimmer of an iridescent lover—everywhere.

—

Had I missed the big shebang? I put down the newspaper and drank a cup of coffee. Then I started sniffing things, old shoes, flaking paint, the little dun-colored dust bunnies beneath my bed. I followed my nose, so to speak, for a day or two, and while it rose to the occasion almost every time, if not with a sneeze, then with a dribble, the rest of my body, well, the rest of my body stayed slack.

And slack, sad to say, is how it usually is on Prozac. Those London ladies are lucky. When Eli Lilly first marketed the drug they reported sexual problems in 1 to 2 percent of users. While estimates of the problem vary widely, some doctors and mental-health professionals now report sexual dysfunction in 40 to 50 percent of their Prozac patients. Think abo it that. If there are twelve million Prozac users worldwide, then six million of them may be impotent, frigid, or otherwise troubled in their sex life. Six million is, by any account, a hefty number. Six million is a number with weight, portent, and loss. Six million were the Jewish Diaspora before World War II. There are six million people on the continent of Australia, in the French countryside, on the coast of Northern California. Six million is a tribe, a race, enough to populate a small and possibly sterile planet.

—

"I am going to write a book," I said to my lover, Bennett, one day, "about Prozac."

"Excellent," Bennett, a chemist, said. "I am always in favor of projects that increase our understanding of drugs."

We were on the couch, my feet in his lap, he stroking my shin, the living room warm with burnished wood and bright fireplace tiles. "What will the chapters be about?" he asked.

"At least one about sex," I said. "Prozac and the erotic."

His hand on my shin stopped. "Will it have us in it?" he asked.

"Who else am I qualified to describe in this arena?" I smiled, paused. "But listen," I said. "I'll show you everything. You can take out the parts you don't like."

"Our sex life, huh?" he said. The room seemed to tilt and tighten, the tendons tensing in our house. Whenever the subject of sex between us came up, the millions of muscles in our world went into spasm. He lifted his hand from my leg now and cupped his chin. "Our sex life, huh?" he said again. He stared at the ceiling. I stared at the ceiling. He looked into the fireplace, which behind its Italian tiles has never been usable, a cold stone cleft.

—

Our sex is not cold. We are gentle and admiring. My Bennett has, for instance, a beautiful mouth. I confess, however, to feeling at times disturbingly distant. I know about the problems that can come with long-term intimacy, the blah sensation when you have traced every nook and link in your lover's body. Believe me, though, the distance of which I speak is different. It is physical. It is local. Boredom is diffuse and psychological. I am not at all bored by Bennett, but it is as though I have been bored into by something else, injected with Novocain at a very specific spot. I want to weep. Sometimes I picture my pelvis as a curved place filled with snow, snow bracketed by bones, eerily pretty in its northern whiteness, where the wind goes.

—

One day, about three years ago, two years into my relationship with Bennett, a comet was coming. I wanted to see this comet. I wanted to feel it flare in me. Scientists were saying its tail of rock and fire would glow in the dark night sky. It was not realistic, but I pictured this comet igniting me from the inside out, star heat in my mouth.

I went outside. The day darkened. I remember the sunset was spectacular that evening, slow and sensual, like a fiery lady dipping into a blue bath.

I lay on the grass and waited. Bennett brought my dinner to the lawn. "Maybe you're just repressed," he had said to me the other night, I who had trouble coming, I who could describe the sensation as nothing else but a delicate mold over my vagina, very thin, and teasingly pink, like the mouth retainers I once wore.

"I will figure this out," I had said, sitting up in bed. "Besides, don't be so goal-oriented. It's not like I don't enjoy you. I'm crazy about you."

But if there's one realm where we want our peaks, it's sex. Stars. Comets. The yard where I lay was surrounded by trees. I stretched on the ground and waited. When the wind moved over me, I lifted my nightshirt to better feel it. Ten o'clock. Eleven o'clock. Bennett leaned out a lighted window two stories above me and said, "All right now. When are you coming in?"

"I haven't seen it yet," I said.

"Forget it," he said. "It's past the time. You missed it."

"No," I said.

"Yes," he said.

"No," I said, insisting on fire and rock.

And so I stayed there, stubborn on the ground, and as I did, and as the night deepened and the trees stood over me like human hulk I could not quite reach, I moved my hands over my bare stomach, letting my fingers mingle in the rough hair that peaks the pubic bone. And then lower, sliding one finger up inside of me, up and up, farther than I had ever gone, until at last I touched the tip of my uterus. I tapped on it once, twice, three times, moving the white wand of my finger like a fairy godmother, spelling myself, blessing myself—*you shall be moist and you shall multiply; tulips will flow in your blood; each pulse of an orgasm will yield a golden coin*. One, two, three, I counted, but I could tell, the wall on which I tapped was numbed, and above me Bennett turned the bedroom light off, and I waited all that night but the comet never came.

—

Some people say sex is not important. My mother used to tell me that sex was something a woman put up with, and that if you counted backward from one hundred or sang to yourself that song about bottles of beer on the wall, you might at least make the trip seem shorter. I am not in agreement with my mother on this point. And it was after the night of the failed comet that I started to really tussle, up front and out loud, with the meaning of this specific thing Prozac had taken from me. To stay on the drug would mean, and continues to mean, that I accept myself as a less sexual being. I am not pleased by this. Even in anorexia I was honoring the centrality of sexuality, insisting with the blade of my body that flesh be noticed, that we grieve its diminishment, that we celebrate the proximity of its crimson innards. And those times, my God, all those jubilant juiced-up raunchy times when I had made such good use of my skin—fifteen, sixteen, eighteen, twelve, lying on my bed, a Sidney Sheldon book propped up on my prepubescent belly, wetness puddling at the base of my vagina, drawing the slickness out until I became a singular sensation, a crest. My God. I can recall my first orgasm at age eight, the sudden surprise of tipping over into new space, new muscles doing new dances, all of it. Through my sexuality I had always felt in contact with an essential self, something unalterably true and female.

And now, the same old story. Lost and found and in the finding still more lost. The ultimate exchange, one essential self for another. On Prozac I have become a barterer, which is for centuries how civilizations have survived and flourished, and also faded.

—

Bartering works when the exchange is even and both sides feel enhanced. Here's the problem with the

Prozac/sex trade-off. I'm not sure it's even or enhancing. After all, there is one thing everyone, from behaviorists with their little Skinner boxes to analysts with their leather couches, seems to agree on. A healthy human adult has a fully functioning sexuality, a sexuality that is not suppressed, repressed, or otherwise damaged. I know of no theorist, from Stack Sullivan and Freud to Horney and Lifton, who would claim it's OK to be, shall we say, dysphoric in the genitals.

Prozac is a strange pill for a lot of reasons, foremost this paradox in its powder. It is a drug hailed as extraordinarily successful in restoring millions upon millions of people to normalcy, and yet, according to the criteria laid out by the doctors who make these claims, on it most people fail in one of the most supposedly central arenas of mental health. A random flip through the *Diagnostic and Statistical Manual of Mental Disorders* (*DSM*) reveals that loss of libido and sexual dysfunction are serious symptoms of several psychological diseases. How are we—no, how am I—to make sense of a pill that more or less brings me to mental soundness and yet, at the same time, turns me away from the lush lands of the sanguine?

And here's another question. How to make sense of a pill that so severs the sexual from the sensual? Prior to Prozac I had always assumed one's sensual and sexual capacities were linked, linked in the cortex, linked in the limbs. We smell, we touch, we taste, we crest, we come. Actions and experiences inseparable. Prozac, however, has taught me that one's sensuality and sexuality are or can be cut. Koskava, my doctor, put it to me this way. "Prozac restores on the general level but punishes on the local level." I agree. Apparently I live on levels, and on Prozac I am less integrated as a human being than maybe I was before. This seems a shame. But let me pause for a moment to look closely at one of my disintegrated levels. Let me creep up from the crotch, swim through the cervix, twine myself around my spiky spinal cord. Let me linger in my fingers, feel the plush pads of my thumbs, and then higher, higher, to the unsheathed eyes, which are bits of naked brain made beautiful in the face. While I am punished I am also graced, and I want you, Bennett, to know, if you read this, which I'm sure you will, that I love you in the physical. I love you as only a lover can. Less depressed, less obsessed, I am better than ever able to love your hair, which has blond lights in it, and your remarkable eyes, the blue of my Nana's chipped china. I love the smell of your skin, impossible to describe except to say it's a confluence of many pungent things, and I love your chest with the disks of your nipples, and your thighs, striated with sweat, and your back and your breath while you are above me. This is the gift of response Prozac has given me, even if I cannot always fully, when you are above me, unwrap the binding ribbons.

—

"I know," Bennett said to me one day, "that there is a way we can fix this."

"How?" I asked.

"Drugs," he said.

"No more drugs," I said. "I'm tanked on enough of this stuff already."

"I don't mean *those* kinds of drugs," he said. "I don't mean drugs from SmithKline, or CVS, or Eli Lilly."

"Look," I said. "If you want me to drop acid, forget it. I've already lost my mind enough times in my life."

"I don't mean acid," he said mysteriously.

"And I'm not doing any mushrooms either, so forget that. I'm not interested in seeing pink elephants in the air."

"I mean herbs," he said.

"Herbs?"

"We are surrounded," he said, "by common plants with amazing chemical properties, which we could extract and make into aphrodisiacs."

"You know how?" I said. "You're sure it's safe?"

"I'm a chemist," he said. "I study this stuff. Of course I know how."

And so off we went, in search of the sensual that might lead to the sexual, corollas and pistils and damp tangled roots in the city's soil.

———

We were in his laboratory, then, with molecular replicas swinging from the ceiling, replicas he had made from piercing gumdrops with toothpicks. On the table, test tubes and scales. We had gathered leaves, the heads of flowers, dark dirty roots. We had the spiny husks of a thorn-apple plant—*Datura ferox,* Bennett called it. He took a small knife and split the spiny casing, like gutting a baby blowfish, and inside globs of wet black seeds, the sudden surprise of caviar, dark and salty. They spilled out on the table, and I reached down, put one in my mouth. "Not yet," he scolded. "We haven't even pre-pared it yet." And he held his palm beneath my chin, and I spit the seed out.

"*Datura ferox,*" he murmured, holding the sphere between thumb and forefinger, where it glinted. I could smell the candy molecules. I could taste the intricate structure of things. A blue-veins beat in my lover's neck, *ta da, ta da ta da.*

"*Datura ferox,*" he murmured again, and then he

scooped all the seeds into a bowl and, with a mortar and pestle, macerated them—*ta da, ta da*—leaning down so hard the shells split, grinding and pounding, pounding and grinding, his lip tight, triceps rising in his arms.

I watched him. Around and around. His lips tight. My eyes stinging. What was it? The odor of crushed seeds, almost oniony? The look on my lover's face, leaning into the problem with all his weight, longing and anger, anger and rage. "Just forgive me, OK?" I wanted to say.

"Don't leave me, OK?" I wanted to say.

"Guava juice," he said.

"What?"

"In the fridge, Lauren," he said, his voice short. "Go get me the guava juice in the fridge. It's part of my recipe."

I opened the apartment-sized fridge in the laboratory and pulled out a can, on its label a picture of a voluptuous Mexican beauty doing the samba.

"Guava juice," I said to him.

"What's wrong?" he said.

"Nothing." I shrugged.

He put down the pestle. "C'mere," he said, slinging one arm around me and pulling me in.

"You should leave me," I said. "You could find someone else better suited to you."

"Who else would put up with me?" he said.

"That's true," I said, because Bennett is a royal slob and a weirdo to boot. He is a thirty-two-year-old man who watches monster movies. He plays a lot of chess. In the summer he wears sarongs.

"Who else?" he said, kissing my neck, "but you?"

—

And then the recipe was ready, thorn-apple mush mixed with Goya guava juice, poured into a shaker with crushed ice, a one-two-three, and then into a cobalt-blue glass, where it frothed and stank.

We were upstairs now, in, of course, the bedroom, and, of course, evening had come on. There were hurricane warnings that night, some storm called Hilda or Barbara slinking along the coast all decked in gauzy clouds and wetness. The glass rattled in the panes. Something crashed on the porch.

"If I die," I said, "all my antiques go to Liza. My money goes to Tracy and Emily. You can have the house."

"You're not going to die," he said. "The mixture's harmless."

"Remember," I said, "my antiques go to—"

"Liza," he said. "And I can have the house. So swallow."

He had a beer. We raised glasses, clinked, and *glub glub glub.*

———

We lay back on the bed in a plume of pillows and a tangle of sheets. We had lit a candle, and it worried the walls, making fretful shadows there. "Feel anything?" he whispered.

I felt something like resin on my lips, and the juice was so powerful that even after half an hour my tongue was still tasty. "Kiss me," I said.

He did, and then I felt something. I felt a sharp stab in my stomach. And bubbles rising. "Jesus," Bennett said, pulling his hand away from my belly, where it had been resting. "What's going on in there?"

"I am in pain," I said, sitting up, but in fact I wasn't anymore. Just one wince and then it was gone. And then came wooziness, sure enough, a gentle melting of the mind and heat in the limbs, along with an overwhelming urge to burp.

Which I did, for the next ten minutes, loud and popping, deep and rumbling, seismic sounds of shifting earth, a coyote's cackle, an owl's howl, burps from the belly and from the hot heart, sounds so amazing that Bennett applauded after each orchestration.

And after each orchestration we laughed and laughed, pulsing contractions that coursed through our bodies, bliss and ache.

—

We tried other aphrodisiacs after that one, mixtures with wonderful names—Vine of the Soul, Semen of the Sun. We trekked around the pond in the early evening, the water there both brackish and sweet. We drank to it, he sharing in the mixtures now, and although none of them worked quite the way they were supposed to, they worked anyway. The mixtures did not bring me to a new place but, rather, revealed to me again and again the place I already was, full of root and egg, touch and guava, a love, like water, both brackish and sweet.

—

"Bartering," I said to myself. "You have made a trade-off, and in the scheme of things it's not too significant. Look at everything you do have."

And I saw and still see everything I do have, but no matter what, there is always the itch of what gets lost. Is there a plant for that?

"I have it too," my friend Rebecca said to me. "Since I've been on the Zac, I just don't feel the same drive."

And by her bedside I saw a squeezed-up tube of Replens moisture cream. "Well," she said, looking at me looking at it. "I guess maybe it's good. I always

162 · Lauren Slater

thought I was oversexed anyway. I'm not too needy for men anymore."

"Sure," I said.

And then later, back at home, I considered her words. That was one way to look at it, Prozac as a feminist tablet, a tablet that makes previously "hungry" women less interested in the corporeal platters laid out by the patriarchy. A tablet that allows women, traditionally seen as nearly bovine in their immanence, to now soar, pure silver and spark, in the quiet, clear space where male geniuses do math and poems.

Consider this: Prozac as a tool of radical feminism, for women who wish to care less in their flesh about men. It is a stretch, yes, but something to ponder, a new tweak on the old drug debate. Previously, critics of Prozac have warned that it aids in social conformity, that it's the ultimately capitalist pill, helping its users shed their dysphoria so that they work more effectively for their corporations and their families, so they drop their deviance, so they produce babies and airplanes with a particularly American glee.

And yet, turn the chemical gem around just a tad, so light shines on its second facet. Now we see not the glint of money and gold furniture wax, but of women, millions of them (60 percent of the twelve million Prozac users are women), who have become indifferent to the mating game, who care less about their bodies in general, who have aged prematurely and celebrate their spinsterhood; *they do not care.* They have silver hair and no makeup. They like to sit on their porches and sip lemonade, or paint their canvases, or observe a spider spin its web, which hangs in the corner of the room and need not be brushed away, a lovely lace doily fluttering there.

So perhaps I have been freed not just from illness but from the shackles of heterosexual sex and all its little conventions. I tried this idea out for a while, and pictured Gloria Steinem becoming the spokesperson for Eli Lilly, her signature on each pill bottle like an athlete's signature on sneakers. It's an idea that interests me, but there are so many flaws in its assumptions that it never quite could comfort me, which is, after all, what I was looking for.

And in the night, when Bennett turns and reaches for me, the idea never quite can comfort me. Often he talks in his sleep. With his eyes open but his brain buzzing in REM, he says wonderful things about me, observing the wings growing out of my back, the coating of silver that surrounds me. Last night, when I came into the bedroom very late, he startled, sat up, blinked his eyes, and said in that sleep-talking voice of his, "Oh my God. Oh my God."

I love conversing with Bennett in this state and confess to even occasionally taking advantage of it, asking
him things like "Have you ever had an affair?" or
"Remember now. Let it sink into your mind. It would
be a good idea to get me a new computer and a belt
sander for my birthday this year."

"Oh my God," he said again, still blinking rapidly.

I stepped toward the bed, shedding my clothes
as I did, reaching for my nightshirt. "What is it?" I
whispered.

"You," he said, his voice somehow harsh and wistful.
His hands were clenched at his sides.

"Me what?" I said.

"You," he said, "are shaped like a droplet."

"Thank you," I said.

He lay back down.

"But," he said, his voice coming right out of the dark,
"you don't flow."

—

My friend Hannah, whom I met during my doctoral
internship and who now lives in Northern California, is
the epitome of flow. She has blond, curly cascades of
hair. She likes to scale rocks and skydive. She is married
but seeks touch outside of that union because her body
is so broad, with so many intricate longings. A graduate
student still, she is writing a dissertation entitled some-

thing like "Subjective Views of Deconstructed Alternative Sexualities." Lately, over the phone, she had been telling me a lot about research for the final chapter on a group of female eunuchs who call themselves the Third Gender, which, they say, is a special sect.

"How can a female be a eunuch?" I asked her. "I thought being a eunuch meant you weren't a man or a woman."

"They call themselves female *and* eunuchs," Hannah said. "I don't know. There's a lot about them I don't understand yet. I need subjects to interview. You should come with me. It could give you some kind of perspective." She paused. "Either that or erotic massage."

"Erotic massage?"

"That could be good for you too. I have an erotic-massage therapist who's so skilled I actually have orgasms in my fingers."

"Uh-huh," I said.

"No, seriously. As soon as your plane lands, I'm taking you."

I would be visiting her in California in a few days, out there for a work conference. "Forget the erotic massage, Hannah. I don't even like undressing for my internist."

"OK," she said. "I can see we need to start you at a less threatening level. Baths."

"Baths," I repeated.

"Northern California is full of them, and some supposedly are pretty popular with this sect. First of all, it's just a great physical experience. Also, who knows who I might meet to interview."

Baths. I pictured pilgrims coming to Lourdes, dunking shriveled limbs in holy water. I pictured baptisms and blessings, oceans and sweet vortexes. I had tried everything else I could think of, save going off the pill, which I would not risk. So now I would try this. A last shot. Baths. Cleansing. Healings. The skin pricked alive at all its points.

—

We drove, her car cutting through the red hills. "This place is called Sounds of Rain," Hannah said. "It's where the eunuchs like to hang."

The baths were underground, a series of steep steps like those you sometimes descend in dreams. And steam, steam and people everywhere. There were women with rolls of fat on their backs, with long feathered earrings and necklaces of pookah beads. The women walked, ambled, knelt, stepped in and out of vaporous tubs, lifted loofahs to their bottoms and sanded themselves. One older lady, with plaits of pure white hair, knelt and rubbed a pumice stone back and forth across her forehead, as though trying to coax back to her a long forgotten word or wish. Steam rose from the tiles and mixed with the smells of soap, sweat, henna, and perfume.

I undressed quickly, covering myself with my arms, and then Hannah and I slipped into a tub. Currents shot out from small spigots in the sides. The froth rose and fell, revealed and concealed, so for one moment you might see the pink of a pierced nipple, or someone's toes.

There were four of us in the tub. I stared at the two unfamiliar faces. I wondered how we were supposed to tell whether or not they were eunuchs. Were we supposed to ask? Did eunuchs look different anyway?

After a while, one of the women, who had a pierced nipple, got up to leave. Now there was just Hannah, myself, and another enormously heavy female with bracelets up to her elbows and a red dot on her forehead. She was not Indian, though, but white, so white, in fact, that she seemed part of the steam. The red dot on her forehead looked like a gem. I stared at it. The dot seemed to sing. I felt an odd buzzing between my legs and behind my eyes. I edged away from her.

"Yes," the woman said, turning to me. "The red mark is magic, and has life forces that can sometimes be experienced as a buzzing in the body."

I eyed Hannah, who, as a native Californian, believes in things like energy circles and chakras. I, a sullen New

Englander, usually had no time for this sort of stuff but, but . . . how did she know I felt a buzzing? Could she read my mind?

"What's the red dot stand for?" Hannah said, gearing up, I could see, into research mode. "I mean, you don't look Indian."

The woman laughed. She was so fat the folds on her throat trembled. For some reason that made me sad. "I am not Indian," she said. "But nor am I American. I exist outside of categories."

"What other categories have you stepped out of?" Hannah said. "If you don't mind my asking." And then she went on to tell the woman she was a graduate student writing a dissertation, et cetera.

The woman, who, it turned out, was one of these female eunuchs and spent at least three hours a day in these baths, meeting here her "sisters and fellow priests," explained her views to us. She saw gender as a socially constructed category, polluting body and mind.

"But how do you get rid of gender?" I asked. "Do you, like, meditate your way out of it?"

"Well, I do meditate," the woman said, "but that's not how I overcame my gender identity. I have had my labia and clitoris surgically removed. Only in that way can I truly have access to the spiritual powers of my priesthood."

"What sorts of spiritual powers?" Hannah asked.

The eunuch went on to tell us how she and others like her are hired out to preside over Indian weddings and births, that, because she exists outside of sex, she has power over it, and so can guide such ceremonies.

Hannah and the eunuch talked about birth and marriage and other significant things. I, however, was absolutely stuck on the more mundane question of what the eunuch actually looked like "down there." I couldn't get my mind off that operation. My God. What, precisely, was left? Neither penis nor vagina. OK, a stretch of blank skin? A single ragged hole, stark and deep? How did she pee? Did she get yeast infections?

"My friend here," Hannah said, "is going through some sexual questions of her own. That's one reason why we came here today. We're looking into alternative views."

"Ahhh," said the priest, turning to me. "Can I be of help?"

I glared at Hannah. In my opinion she had questionable boundaries.

"Oh, no," I said. "I'm fine, thank you. It's all been very interesting, though, and it was good to meet you."

"Good to meet both of you," the priest said, and then, with no more ado, she stood up, plowing through the water, shaking rivulets off her shoulders, flinging droplets from her knotted hair, the whole bath heaving with her tidal movements.

And for just a moment she stood before us, shed of the fabric of water, utterly visible, so I could have maybe seen the space between her thighs, a cold crotch or a pit of possibility. She faced me, mammoth, the sagging shelf of her breasts, and it was only there I dared to look, at the wizened nipples with dark hairs around them, a second set of eyes, black-lashed and bloodshot. Ugly.

—

We lay in silence for several minutes after she had left. I thought to chastise Hannah for embarrassing me, but suddenly I was just too tired, and she was my friend and meant well. Alone, just the two of us now in the tub, we let the water lap over us. "Wow," Hannah finally said. "Some chick."

"Yeah," I muttered, and stared up at the ceiling, where drops of condensation formed. I fixed my eyes to a drop and watched it closely. It quivered and swelled, hung like a tiny teat, filling and then finally falling.

My eyes felt wet, from the humidity. And the ugliness. It was probably nearing four o'clock, time for my next dose.

"Let's go," I said.

But we didn't move. We lay there just a little longer.

For no matter what, the water here was warm, and the spigots pulsed continuously on our backs, awakening the spinal nerves at many levels. Late in the day now, the bath began to empty of almost everyone, and soon the room was almost perfectly quiet, allowing me to hear better than ever the licking of waves, the padding of bare feet on stone. And behind those sounds, or above them, I imagined music and charred bones from some Indian festival. She was there, and I could see. A pyre. An Indian sky with a rounded church dome glowing like a nipple against the setting sun. Gardens where there was jasmine, and boys with loincloths suggesting naked buttocks beneath. Someone moaned. A huge contraction came as a woman gave birth. Her hands steady, the priest, the one with no holes or five holes, guides the baby's head into the light. She watches the new mother writhe, and later, standing by a marriage bed, she blesses the red drop that falls from the virgin. She is calm and composed, always. Big and bland in her body, she is strong as a spent volcano. It was, I thought, my last chance here in these baths. Maybe, just maybe, I could learn to see her as she saw herself.

And so, sometimes, I practice. I fill the tub at home with water and lower myself down. I pretend there is nothing between my thighs, which, you would think, given my situation, should be quite easy, but it is not. For there is, most definitely, something, and the more I try to make it disappear, the more it insists on making itself known, with itches and little fitful sparks. This is what psychologists call a paradoxical response, and I consider it a gift from the priest, who, perhaps, without my knowing, was psychologist par excellence. I think of her often. I think of her when I imagine some sexy scene and the sparks will not quite catch. Later, alone in the bedroom, Bennett still at work, I tell myself what I imagine she might tell me: that I am of a cooler and a lighter hue. I am a beautiful blue so pale it suggests vapor and yet also hints at a deepness it cannot quite reveal. In these ways I can comfort myself, until Bennett comes home and reaches for me and my images fail, and I remember loss. Then I have this to ask. Please keep reaching. We may yet find a plant. Or we may come to terms. No matter what our gaps and amputations, we are alive. The priest is alive. Bennett and I, well, we are also alive, and have decided, in a way both brackish and sweet, to marry, and we do what families for centuries have done, hunting and gathering, extracting spotted flowers from the earth, with a trowel and a shovel midwifing the wonders and then, in grief, folding them back under, doing our burying work.

8. Identify patient strengths by underlining from the following list: <u>intelligence</u>; <u>motivation</u>; strong support system; <u>capacity for insight</u>; <u>humor</u>; ability to form positive interpersonal connections; ability to use good judgment; cohesive work history; <u>educational background</u>; optimistic—

Our bodies grew lovely and bloody as we entered our thir-teenth year. We were horse girls, camp girls, and every dawn we went to the barn to see the hides steaming thickly in summer dawns. "Che che Chigger," Kimberly, our counselor, would say as she ran her hands down the muscular buttocks of a rope-tied thoroughbred. "My Chigger," she would say in those mornings, "my beauty, my blackness, my love." Out of her grooming basket came the shears, the currying comb, the hoof pick. We would watch Chigger jolt and lower his head, feel him mouth our palms with his loose velvety lips that left no trace of their wetness. Silence in the stable except for the big breathing of the horses and whisk of the currying comb, strapped to the back of Kimberly's hand, making its way over the matted fur, under the belly, and at last to the tight blue bags of the stallion's testicles.

Chigger had twice the blood, four times the fire of an ordinary gelding, and I wanted to ride him as beautifully as Kimberly could. But I was afraid of his hard angular head and his body's mesh of angled bones. I was afraid of many things that summer, although I did not show it. I was popular and scrappy, and no one knew how I feared the other girls, the counselors, myself, standing on the brink of a brand-new body I could not understand.

Alone, away from the other girls, I lay in the cabin and touched myself, the black sprouts of hair and the inner parts of me that seemed to flare on my fingers. I filled out and softened. I ambled and tripped.

"You girls," Kimberly would shout at us during lessons. "You girls have no grace. Don't flop all over your saddles. Don't clutch at the reins for balance. Heels down. I said, HEELS DOWN, SLATER," and she'd come to me, push my leg into proper position.

One day, when Kimberly had had enough of our sloppy riding styles, she went into the center of the ring and set the jump at four feet high. "Now," she said. "I want you to cross *your stirrups and tie your reins. A rider, a* person, *has to learn to depend on inner balance. Inner," she said, tapping her trim belly. "Go ahead. Do as I say." We slid our feet from the stirrups and made loose leather knots with our reins. The sun was so hot, tossing a gloss on the field and the fence, making the cabins of the campsite look unreal, as though they did not exist and there would be no safe place for me to go. One by one each girl cantered up to the jump and, as though transformed by this pressure to perform, flew over it in perfect poise, hands clasped behind her head, legs fastened to the horse's flanks. "Good, good," Kimberly said. Then it was my turn. "Go on, Silva," I whispered, but my horse felt my fear; he raced toward the fence, hesitated, bunched to a scuttering halt. "Again!" Kimberly ordered, and I tried again, urging him onward, my legs pressed close to the horse's hot sides, but again—my fear—and again the gelding shied. "If you can't do it right," Kimberly shouted, "then I'll really make it wrong for you."*

After four tries, Kimberly brought Chigger out from his free roam in the field, saddled him, and said, "Try this, Slater." I got astride the stallion's back. Immediately I felt the energy, different from any other horse I'd ever been on, a tremble and a flow, as though I held between my legs not a horse but an ocean of blood and loose-limbed kelp and shiny black waves that sang in their roll and dash. Chigger sidestepped impatiently, thrust his head down, clanked the bit in his teeth. I remembered his teeth in the barn darkness, even, sharp as sharks', streaks of green staining the ivory enamel. Chigger snorted, backed up, and before I could turn him toward the fence took the most elegant, stinking dump I'd ever seen from horse or human before, six firm, squarish hunks like precious stones pulled steaming from a pink cave. The dump lay there, beautiful, black, wet on the ground. I didn't want to stop looking at it. I didn't want to stop smelling it, the loveliest sight I'd seen since coming to camp that summer. I wanted to step in it. I wanted to sleep in it. I wanted to do something with my body as elegant and sure of itself as that shit was.

"Come on, Slater," Kimberly shouted.

"Without my reins?" I squeaked. "Without my stirrups?"

"Without a thing," she said. "Except yourself and your beast."

In extreme anxiety your pupils narrow; your sight goes dim. I saw very little but I felt it all. I kept my feet pressed close to the stallion's sides. I buried my hands in the maze of black mane. I aimed Chigger toward the fence and let him do the rest, let him lift me, water, wave, blood of my blood; we rose, linked in a single leap, and I felt, for the first time, like a part of something beautiful. It was only for a moment, but in the air I was elegant—oh, supple person pulled hot, pulled strong, from the skin of her own fears.

Ten years have gone by now since I started the drug. Sometimes my hands shake. Last night I felt an odd flutter in my eyes. I know Prozac can sometimes have long-term side effects, but because it is still relatively new on the scene, researchers can't say exactly what those side effects may be. Searching the Web, I meet Prozac users who claim the medication has caused low blood sugar, irregular eye movements, weight gain, and God knows what other assortment of ills. I have learned that Prozac has one of the longest half-lives of any medication available. It takes forty-eight hours to excrete just a portion of its chemical metabolites. Like uranium, Prozac glows underground, in the private darkness of our flesh, in the body's bowel, in the deep tissue of lung, both ominously and beautifully radiant.

Lately I have become especially concerned about Prozac and memory. I used to be able to read a paragraph and recite back its phrases in near-perfect order. I never before needed an appointment book. I admit, I am older now. However, I am not so old that I should frequently forget the names of towns I've lived in, streets I've roamed, dishes I have always savored. People I have loved. Gaps in my cognition are appearing, places where the denim is worn so thin the skin shows through.

At night I have this dream. Above me a capsule turns and shines like a planet. I am in the neighborhood where I now live, only it has become absolutely unfamiliar to me and I cannot find my way home. I know my home is somewhere near here, up that hill, around that corner, but the memory of place and points of reference has vanished. Panicked, I look in lit and darkened windows. I struggle to recall, and feel the knowledge of my home on the tip of my tongue, like a name, like a love. The streets are shadowy, and always there are jack-o'-lanterns with fires in their smiles. A person comes up the street. I plan to ask her where my home is, but as she approaches I feel myself forgetting the question bit by bit, so first the word *where* goes, and then the word *is,* and *my,* and at last, to my horror, *home; home,* so I can say nothing, so I can have nothing, so I live nowhere and, drugged dumb, I cannot even question.

—

Given my questions, maybe it would be wiser if I stopped the drug. Actually, I have tried several times. I decrease my dosage slowly, inching down day by day, and then I cease altogether. Or I forget to take my dose one day, and then again the next, and by the time I have remembered I think, *What the hell, let's see what happens.* I picture myself drug-free, managing my life, and I get a jolt of joy. Sometimes, in the movie theater or the supermarket, I look around at people who I suppose live their lives without a chemical crutch, and they amaze me. There is a woman with a yellow scarf knotted around her neck. The yellow is the color of corn, of sunflowers, and she herself seems to have sprung from some garden. There are the children on the street. *To live without a drug.* After so many years, that to me is like living without water, something I cannot imagine, and the people who do this have a certain stature in my eyes.

And it's because I want this stature, and because I am fearful of the as-yet-undiscovered side effects, that I try to do without. "How long will I have to be on the antidepressant?" so many patients ask their doctors. The answers vary with the doctors, but some say that, after a while, Prozac corrects your brain chemistry and even without it you continue to function well enough. So I go from four pills to three. Three to two. Two to one, and a half, and a quarter. Blastoff.

I always break up. Maybe not at first. There have been a few weeks, even once more than a month, when I soared through space and saw the stars as peaceful. But each time, eventually, there's a little splitting sound and then a big *kaboom,* and the wreckage is a mess. Last time I tried going off Prozac I became obsessed with dogs. I spent six hundred dollars on books about dogs, their breeds and temperaments, and I am now familiar with every AKC pup from akitas to whippets. Sad to say, I skipped work for more than a few days to up my erudition. Driven behavior has an educational component, no doubt, but I am not a vet and never plan to run a kennel, and such canine-focused learning seemed, to say the least, a little out of place in the life of a psychologist.

Also, it's exhausting for Bennett. "Sometimes," he said to me a few months ago, "you run your life like it's an emergency. I'm going to put a fire pole from the third floor to the first floor so you can slide right down it and skip the stairs."

Dogs and fire poles, nicks in the skin and the brightness of blood—all in all, life is easier thanks to my good friends Eli and Lilly. I know I can do it without them— my experiences have shown me how I might find dignity even in the hottest of illnesses. But there is no doubt that Eli and Lilly are lovely folks, well dressed and mild-mannered, and to live with them is to live in a place where a brook babbles and many flowers grow, and the windows, although they rattle in their panes, do not shatter in storms.

"So take the pills," Bennett says to me. "Everyone's dependent on chemicals in one way or another to function. Some people are even dependent on ASA's."

"ASA's?"

"Aspirin," he said. "No kidding. There's hard-core documentation that aspirin dependence is a problem for a lot of people."

"I don't want to be drug-dependent," I say.

"Well, you probably are," he says. "And it doesn't have to be a devastating thing, although that's the way it's portrayed. There are plenty of addicts who lead perfectly respectable lives."

"An addict?" I say. "You think so?"

—

What does it mean, even, to be an addict? The *DSM IV* calls addiction a state marked by tolerance and continued use despite substance-related problems, say, sexual dysfunction, odd kinks in cognition, a tremor here and there. Addiction and dependency—I am using them interchangeably—are also characterized by an individual's unsuccessful attempts to cut down or eliminate the substance from her life. My life. Me.

Bennett's father, Bruce Alexander, is a psychologist, and in his book *Peaceful Measures,* he defines dependency as occurring when users show diminished flexibility in their behavior toward a particular drug, and also when they act as though the effects of the drug are necessary to their well-being. He would also argue for a distinction between the concepts of addiction and dependency, believing that a person can be dependent without being addicted, for addiction is marked by an overwhelming psychological involvement with the substance, while dependency can exist as a dull but drumming need in the background of one's life.

In the field of drug studies there is considerable debate over terms like *addiction* and *dependence* and the delicate distinction between the two. While I tip my hat to this debate, I take a blunter approach to things. You are an addict, in my mind, if you feel compelled to consistently consume something you wish you wouldn't, and if that something exists outside the basic requirements of your central nervous system. The something

can be "good." The something can be "bad." The something can "enrich" or the something can "diminish."
What it measurably does in one's life is less important
than one's persistent and uncomfortable sense of servi-
tude or even slavery.

———

I am drug-dependent, then, yet another unforeseen
side effect. Whereas once, a long time ago, I had an illness identity, I now have an addict identity, and this
does not sit well with me. In attempting to ameliorate
one medical condition, I have stumbled upon another,
an iatrogenic injury. But maybe that's not the real problem. Maybe the real problem is this. Above the entrance
to my elementary school there was a stone engrav-
ing, beautiful cursive letters hewn from granite—
AUTONOMY ABOVE ALL ELSE—an angel etched at each
end of the phrase giving the whole thing the appearance
of a heavenly message, a mandate sent straight from the
sky. Later on, when I was in graduate school, the developmental theories we studied all hunkered around the
concept of autonomy as the peak of human potential.
Even the gardening books I read reveal their biases, cel-
ebrating the pink and yellow cosmos for the toughness
and suppleness of their stems, the painted ladies that
grow back year after year, pushing their skulls through
the rime of frost and earth's decay to flame in the

wettest or driest of weather, Olympian torches of tulips.

If I were a flower, I would probably be an orchid, for orchids are pretty plants whose florid surfaces—stripes and dots—go a long way toward hiding their parasitic nature, the way they leech off other plant life, the very particular conditions they require in order to flourish. But I am not an orchid, of course; I am most definitely a person. As a person, I picture myself as young, sometimes very young, suckling my pills, which are shaped like tiny teats. I take in my nourishment. Like mother's milk, it builds my strength, facilitates the nerve growth in my brain, so my dendrites sprout longer, my axons curl and clutch at new connections, and the soft spot in my head hardens, and hardens again. Dr. Peter Kramer would argue that, due to all this superior nutrition, Prozac has increased my autonomy, broadening my range of motion. True, my life is wider now, as wide as the splaying and spectacular orchid's cup, but look below that level, and you will see how I am. I am linked, hooked at the hip, stitched in the skin to a primordial relationship, to Eli and Lilly, who rock me and feed me and, late at night, come to my bedside and sing me songs that disturb my sleep and descend to the deepest level of dreams that are not quite mine.

—

"But," says Bennett, "you have to consider drug use in other cultures. Your shame about being drug-dependent is very American."

I go to the library then, both his and the public one in Cambridge, and look through the collections. I find accounts of opium dens in the East, perfectly legal enclaves, where carved pipes emit sweet smoke, where eyes go glazed and the calmest of hands move ivory chess pieces across a board blurred black and red. These denizens of the den are, according to the books I read, responsible proletariat who, in the dawn hours, work successfully to feed a family. Their dependencies are not a secret. Their pipes are not shameful stems but intricately carved pieces of wood or, better yet, bone, through which the smoke flows and fills.

There are the Waiká Indians of South America, who regularly depend on the hallucinogenic properties of the area's plants to put them in touch with their gods, making and ingesting an intoxicant called *epená,* which is dangled from a long bamboo tube and is available for constant snuffing. Andrew Weil, in his book *The Natural Mind,* writes, "Dependence . . . if stable, can be consistent with social productivity. . . . Stable users are psychologically mature individuals."

Yes.

No. (Those tiny teats.)

So, we all have our teats. We all suckle something or other.

I am a Waiká Indian, a Chinese in an opium den. I am in the Amazon, and as I down my milk, the culture claps and dances.

Maybe I am dancing. Maybe I am dancing my way into some truth or, as I sometimes suspect, scrambling along the steps of researched rationalization, which, thank God or perhaps Prozac, I am solidly sane enough to do.

—

Drug dependency carries its own shameful stigma, but the stigma deepens, I think, if the substance upon which one relies is considered potentially bionic. We know insulin, estrogen, lithium, and Clozaril restore the person to a more or less normal state. A menopausal female's daily dose of Premarin does not transform her into a Superwoman, making her breasts rosy, drops of milk on the firm tips, her fallopian tubes so rich in eggs that they spill into the interior curves of her hips so that from her ripe body whole generations grow. No. She takes that little estrogen pill and manages, at best, to avoid vaginal parchedness and hot flashes that might otherwise plague her. A diabetic's pancreas does not double in size and strength when he takes his insulin. A whopping one quarter of the world's population is born with or develops vision deficiencies, which lenses of various thicknesses can fix.

However, if the good eye doctor gave to the myopic a pair of glasses, say, with diamond-studded rims and lenses made of a mysterious mica that allowed the lucky user to see the molecules in the air, the quarks in the ground, to see to the lowest level of our earth, where the molten core simmers, and then to the farthest fringes of space, we might, after pausing to take in some interstellar information, want to confiscate such a cure from the patient. Or at the very least, we would have some problems with the implications of such glasses. What bounty would those lenses bring to the wearer? Could it be that he might see more deeply into us, penetrating not only the sky but our very skins to eke out our secret thoughts? Could it be that the Turks might get a hold of him and use his powers to flush the Kurds from their hiding places in rocky cliffs on the Turkish border? In a competitive world, advantage for one means death for another, and so those glasses, while bringing life closer, could also crush it out.

And herein lies the problem with Prozac. Some people suspect, perhaps correctly, perhaps not, that users are dependent on a drug that does not so much rehabilitate as transform beyond some physiologically appropriate baseline state. I am both fascinated and bothered by this possibility, and no matter how much I think about the issue, I can come to no conclusion. I see both sides. Peter Kramer, in *Listening to Prozac,* has probably been the most influential proponent of one side of the theory, claiming Prozac is "cosmetic psychopharmacology," that it not only removes symptoms but transforms or possibly transmogrifies the essence of personality, making users "better than well," inducing "mental agility" where before there was none, imparting confidence to the timid, optimism to the habitually pessimistic, flexibility to the rigid of habit. Kramer is unequivocal in his belief that Prozac is the Elizabeth Arden of psychopharmacology, a veritable chemical "makeover," a term that implies trickery and shadow, an artful application of powders and creams to hide unsightly blemishes. In short, makeovers are masks that play with depth and space and dimples, at their very least creating cuteness where before there was none.

It is one thing to be dependent on a drug, but the issues get more thorny still if the substance imparts unfair advantage. Thus I wonder, am I now entering the wrestling ring of life on psychic steroids? Thinking of it this way, I feel not only the shame of dependency but the guilt of chicanery, and this, for sure, is yet another issue inherent in a long-term liaison with Prozac.

True, I am captivated by Kramer's thesis, but I am not so quick to submit to it entirely. In his book Kramer gives example after example of people with low-grade depressions and vague compulsive styles who, upon ingesting Prozac, are absolutely transformed beyond anything resembling their original self. While it is a fact that Prozac, at least in my case, had strong transformative powers in the beginning, it rather quickly, to use the phrase of the medical community, "pooped out," the stilts shrinking to fine high heels on my best days, on my worst days to stunted flats. Would Kramer, I wonder, have written a different book if he had followed his subjects over a long-term, say, five- or ten-year period, the time it takes for tolerance to develop and the person to make sense of such a shock?

More important, the radical transformations of which Kramer writes are, to my mind anyway, problematic in their very essence. The miracle of Prozac, according to Kramer, is that for whatever time or however inconsistently, it imparts to people powers and proclivities not true to their personality. The issue of tolerance aside, I wonder how Kramer can know that the habitually dysthymic patients he treated, the ones who responded to Prozac with surges of optimism and pragmatism, did not possess such qualities as elements of their "original selves." Kramer relies on self-reports to come to the conclusion that low-grade depression and pessimism were, in fact, always parts of his patients' lives. However, subjective self-reports, especially when they draw on memories of things far past, and when they are colored by a person's present pain, are unreliable, to say the least. Thus, it could be that the optimism and pragmatism supposedly imparted to his patients by Prozac were really relics of some original self, relics buried under the detritus of depression, tarnished now to green.

I don't know because I've never met any of the subjects Kramer writes about in his book, and even if I did know them now, I certainly did not know them in their early lives, in their early selves, in the prenatal hints of genetic or God-given potentials that perhaps got lost along the way. However, I do know myself, at least somewhat. Prior to Prozac, when asked to describe my early history, I would tell a story of depression with roots so far-reaching even my earliest memories came up gray. I would tell about the girl on the porch, listening to the *tip tap tap* of her mother's footsteps in an air-conditioned house where frost seemed to form on the coverings of the couch, and that girl, stuck outside in the summer heat, would be picking at skin in search of sensation. I would tell of a mull of whiteness and then the simmer of humiliation, and early on, the sound of voices within me.

These things are true to me. But, having been on Prozac for ten years now, I notice my memory of my early life changing a bit. I still vividly recall the whiteness, the fear, the cold, the cuts. But the lifting of illness, incomplete though it is, has brought other, more colorful glints as well. In altering my present sense of who I am, Prozac has demanded a revisioning of my history, and this revisioning is, perhaps, the most stunning side effect of all.

It has gone something like this. One day, years into my Prozac career and after a particularly rewarding job promotion, I was walking through downtown Chelsea. I was elated. I saw my reflection skimming by in the windows of buildings, and then I recalled being ten years old and standing on a pond of ice in a pair of new skates. It was the dead of winter, and the nude trees were absolutely black-branched in the silver air. My mother was at the edge of the pond, an elegant scarf wrapped around her neck, her hands heated in an angora muff. I had sharpened my skates earlier, and now, as I started to move, I could hear the frosty sound of my blades shaving away at the ice, faster and faster, a quick crouch, a nimble leap, I entering the air in a spin.

She clapped and clapped, and although, later on, she did not draw me close, she said, "You are a girl with know-how."

Walking through Chelsea that day, I was that girl, her memory suddenly returned to me. I had know-how, my mother told me so, only that little tendency, that fact and firmness, had gotten buried in a gnarled mess. In the months that followed, other facts came back, facts I had always forgotten to tell psychiatrists, to tell the nurses at the hospital, to tell, most important, myself. There was, for instance, the fact that Barbar Jean called me Chief, the fact that every year until the age of twelve, when, as Carol Gilligan might say, I lost my "voice," I was elected class president. I was leader of the band. I loved the grapes growing in wild brambles in the woods, dark gems of fruit amid thickly lobed leaves, the taste of pectin on my tongue. I loved horses and the smell of tack soap in a barn, the feeling of a broad warm back beneath me, and when I rode, I jumped fences four feet high. I had a special fondness for a horse named Chigger, who was, of course, a stallion, a magnificent animal with a shiny coat and blue bags for testicles, who champed the bit in his soft red mouth and soared in his gallop so fast he absorbed you in his muscle. I feared him and adored him, and while the other children opted for geldings, I came, after a while, to insist on him. A brave girl. A lost girl. A sad girl. A strong girl. All, all of these things, never woven, told as separate stories.

Jung has a theory of what he calls essential self. Like so much of Jung, it is a theory tinged with mysticism. James Hillman, a contemporary psychologist, has continued Jung's theory, wondering if, beneath all the mutability of postmodernism, there does not exist some core, some calling, and the task of psychotherapy, or treatment in general, is not to expand the self but to peel away at it until the original nubs, perhaps pieces of bone or shiny knobs of rock, emerge. It could be that Prozac is a conduit to one or some of those nubs, a kind of psychotropic Drāno clearing the congestion so the shine is visible. There. There it is.

If this is the case, then, when I take Prozac, I am not being made over so much as I am being remembered. I am not coming upon a new self so much as rediscovering pieces of the old, the girl in the glass case, the blue baby, coming alive now, touching words and air. Some writers, William Styron among them, talk about the importance of alcohol in loosening up the lids of memory and imagination, alcohol as an aid to narrative creation, to the making of stories true and resonant. Prozac may be similar in that, by removing inhibiting symptoms, it allows the self to find a more robust and accurate history to support its present plot and theme. Without the pill, my conviction in that history fails me. My memory fails me. The old arthritis comes back, and I cannot reach the nub. I stiffen in spasm, and then, after years, I forget fluidity was ever once mine.

Or maybe not. Like I said, I can see both sides. I find flaws in Kramer's assertions, but I cannot entirely dispel them. I am also aware of the possibility that on the days Prozac works for me, the days when I am free of obsession and depression, I am powered beyond me, pushed into a realm where unfair advantage becomes mine. "I wish I was sick enough to take that stuff," my friend Susan sometimes says to me. "You're one of the most amazingly productive people I know."

I have two responses to Susan's statement, both defensive. It could be that my "amazing" productivity (completion of a doctoral program in two years, becoming a psychologist, director of the clinic where I now work, lecturer, writer, and furniture refinisher) is not so much due to my partial "cure" but to the experience of illness, of incapacitating OCD, which still sometimes cripples me, and the full-time return of which I fear to the point of nightmares. My firsthand knowledge of psychological paralysis and death, and the sense I have that they may return, means I must move, move now, grasp whatever I can, take in time as though it were in short supply. Which it is. Hungry and grateful, I feast.

And to Susan I also want to say, "See. See me. This isn't just Prozac. Or all Prozac. I am the girl whose hands are stained with purple juice, who spins over ponds, who is hock and horse as she jumps. I am lather."

But I don't tell her about these things. I am not so sure. The girl on skates, I did not dream her, but she could be an aberration, born in moments of serendipitous grace, with only the loosest links to me. If so, then I am sorry for my dependence, because I don't think it's right to ingest psychic steroids. I can blame our culture and say that, all in all, if we were less competitive, then steroids and strength would not be such an issue. That sits well cerebrally but not in my gut. No one wants to be dependent, but more than that, no one wants to be a cheater. No one wants to be a fake.

—

"Oh, please," my friend Ian says to me. He has a red mustache and smokes a pipe, little puffs spicing the air around him. He teaches at MIT, and he's well versed in Derrida, Lacan, Adorno, in postmodern concepts that claim authentic identities are illusory remnants of the romantic age and that the truth is no truth at all. "All of this brooding," he says to me one night as we sit on his rust-colored couch, in his contemporary house where art all gray angles and lines hangs on the white walls. "You're thinking too much about a real self. At the very least, it's passé. The real self as a belief went out in the seventies."

From an academic point of view, he's right. Why worry about whether or not I'm addicted to a substance that makes me inauthentic when every university worth its salt has trashed authenticity anyway? The essence of postmodernism is, in the words of cultural critic Kenneth Gergen, "a world where anything goes that can be negotiated. . . . Selves as possessors of real and identifiable characteristics, such as rationality, emotion, inspiration and will—are dismantled."

Those who are comfortably dependent on Prozac may be, in part, those who have consciously or not embraced a postmodern sensibility, who believe that the ideals of objectivity and truth are outmoded and impossible. I, however, am not one of those people. If Ian and I were discussing authenticity in my house, we would be sitting in a one-hundred-year-old living room, surrounded by pieces of furniture I have scavenged from trash piles, because I am a person who at worst is prone to nostalgia, at best believes that roots are real, and that they demand from us commitment and care. I am also a person who very likely, sad to say, has an entrenched hierarchical sense of things, so that extreme relativism, one idea being just as good as another, does not appeal to me. I cannot help but think some ideas are better than others, that not all perspectives are equal in worth, even while a part of me admires the humility born from such postmodern egalitarianism. I don't think people should ever have such hubris as to state they possess the golden measuring stick, but for myself anyway, I try to have the heart to approximate what I imagine its increments might be.

So. There it is. Here I am. Or here I am not. The difference really matters to me. Probably, despite the trends in our universities, it matters to a lot of people. It could be that many people will continue to believe in bedrock or, better yet, to believe in the importance of the search. The search for the genuine. The gem.

A long time ago my mother, a most elegant woman, took me with her to a jewelry store. I saw rubies blazing on pads of velvet and brooches barnacled with diamonds. My mother was looking for pearl jewelry. The saleslady showed us her wares, placing on the glass counter nacreous bulbs of various sizes, this one with a blue tinge, this one with the slightest haze of pink, this one fat and shaped like a raindrop, this one as petite as a punctuation point. My mother fingered them all, holding the globes up to the light, turning them left, now right. She squinted her eyes to study the filigreed settings of gold, the loops of necklaces and bracelets with tiny clasps. "One hundred and twenty-five dollars," the saleslady murmured in answer to my mother's question; "three hundred dollars; oh, that one there, it's quite fine. A bit over a thousand, I think."

I reached out to touch the pearls' pale curves. I didn't understand. A hundred dollars. Two hundred dollars. All pretty, yes. Maybe even beautiful. The precise color of the moon's penumbra, or of a newborn's fingernail. But still, next door at the CVS my mother could buy just as many pearl pieces that looked just exactly the same—barrettes of pearl, earrings made of pearl clusters, pearly headbands and pearl-handled combs—for ninety-nine cents apiece, and absolutely no one would know the difference.

"The teeth know the difference," my mother said. "Even if the eye can't tell what's real, the mouth can," and she explained to me then how, by tapping a pearl against your molars and mesials, you could tell, by sound and texture and, I've always imagined, by the faint trace of a salty taste, whether it came from the heart of a living oyster or from something else. It was the oyster we wanted. It was the thing inside the scaly shell, the stone from the center of the ocean where the minerals that sustain us are made. And it was the mouth, the most sensitive part of the body, the cavern where nerve endings are covered by the barest haze of skin, that would always crave a true taste.

Sometimes, now, when I look at my Prozac capsules, I think of my mother and myself in that jewelry store. I sit in my kitchen, in the house Bennett and I have been able to buy, a stamp of sun set solidly in the middle of the waxed pine floor. It is still too early to leave for work, but my briefcase is packed, my pumps polished. My dog, with his deep copper coat, rests himself on the wood, and the morning air holds the scent of coffee and yeast. I lift the pill bottle from the windowsill. Outside in the garden I have learned to grow, the peas are getting fat. They are straining against their girdled pods. The cosmos are huge, tall pink cups of light. I imagine my mother is walking out there, in the rich black beds where jewels bloom. "How much," I hear her say, "does it cost?" *How much,* I say to myself, *has it cost?* It is morning now, morning yet again, and I shake one capsule from the bottle. I stare into the pearl of the pill and wonder whether it has given rise to an addiction that brings me closer to my oystery heart or further from it, a barnacle stuck on the exoskeleton of a shell. Like my mother, I hold the gem up between thumb and forefinger, turning it this way, turning it that, assessing how light lands on its surface, pushes to illuminate the sphere's interior, where, I sometimes imagine, my whole world might live, *a long long time ago there once was*—a hospital, a nurse, a horse, a love. A scalpel sharp enough to sever or to stitch. I picture it all inside the pill, which is pearl and nipple, which makes me so many many metaphors, and finally, then, I am grateful. My cognition may be fraying, my libido may be down, I may lose language. Prozac is a medicine that takes much away, but its very presence in my life has been about preserving as well as decaying. The flowers I cure. About remembering as well as forgetting. The pond and a pair of skates. In the dream I forget the word *where,* I forget the word *home,* but in my waking life Prozac has taken me deeper and deeper into those questions—me or not me, crutch or inner bone. Returned, I am then, with each daily dose, with the wash of water to take the pill down, returned I am to my stomach, to my skin, to the fabrics of my past and, yes, to the threat of the synthetic. This is Prozac's burden and its gift, keeping me alive to the most human of questions, bringing me forward, bringing me back, swaddling and unswaddling me, pushing me to ask which wrappings are real.

I have only this left to say.

There was once a girl who liked to cast her rod at a pond behind her house. Stocked, that pond was, with carp and trout, pollywogs and minnows; each time she filled her bucket with the silver slipperiness of fish, all of which she threw back before they died.

And then one day the girl caught a huge fish, with whiskers. He rose slowly out of the water, his mouth crisp with blood, his orange body glowing like a lantern. As long as her leg, this fish was, special, for sure; she had to eat him. The girl thought it was wrong to kill, but she also wanted to. When she took the fish home her father looked impressed and her mother, well, her mother brought the knife. The girl then slit the fellow from fin to tail, opened him up, and saw his heart. She saw a lot of brown gunk. She saw a drop of warm red on her mother's shiny shoe.

"Look what he's got in his stomach," her father said.

The girl leaned down close, and then she saw a blue shard in the fish's stomach, a piece of plastic he had somehow managed to swallow. She picked it up and held it in her hand. The girl was only seven, but already the deadness in her was deep. So she decided to pretend this piece of plastic was a magic pill, and she was cupping it. "Well," her father said, "I'm surprised the fish survived for as long as he did with that thing in him. You shouldn't feel bad about killing him because he was probably slowly dying anyway."

Dying. Slowly. Swallowed.

But maybe not. Maybe, the girl thought, the plastic pill was a special secret vitamin a very skinny lady had accidentally dropped off the side of her boat. Then the fish had gotten the pill, and he had grown huge in health. She didn't know if that fish was monstrous or miraculous or both.

When no one was looking, the girl slipped the blue medicine into her pocket. Its smell was strong—rot and rawness. And that night she hid it beneath her pillow, and then she dreamt she fed it to her mother. She dreamt she slipped it into her mother's coffee, and her mother started to choke. The girl, swallowing the pill now, also started to choke, and a beautiful fish grew in her—grows in her still—larger and larger she gets, a powerful thrust that both stifles and propels——Prozac——

Dying. Slowly. Swallowed.

But the sea is lovely today.

In the balance of things, Doctor, this girl thanks you for your help.

She thanks you——I thank you——for the fish, the growth, the sadness, suspension.

Here I hang, my skin all silver, my mouth pierced on this precious hook.

A PENGUIN READERS GUIDE TO

PROZAC
DIARY

Lauren Slater

AN INTRODUCTION
TO *PROZAC DIARY*

Lauren Slater wakes up one morning to find "the world as I had known it my whole life did not seem to exist." The commonplace things in her scruffy, barely furnished basement apartment and the familiar scene outside her kitchen window have been transformed, smoothed out, slowed down. The "nattering need to touch, count, check, and tap, over and over again"—a manifestation of the obsessive-compulsive disorder that has controlled her life—has disappeared. For Slater, each transformation represents a small miracle. At the age of twenty-six, after five incarcerations in mental hospitals "pursuing and pursued by one illness after another," she is experiencing the world from a healthy perspective for the first time in years. A pioneer patient in an era of cutting-edge psychopharmacology, Slater owes her miraculous awakening to Prozac. Released on the market by Eli Lilly in 1988, Prozac promised to revolutionize the treatment of everything from chronic depression to anorexia to OCD. As Slater's doctor proudly put it, it "was a drug with the precision of a Scud missile, launched miles away from its target only to land, with a proud flare, right on the enemy's roof."

In *Prozac Diary,* a rich and beautifully written memoir, Slater describes what it is like to experience the heady high of Prozac's bright flare, to spend most of your life feeling crazy and then to find yourself in the strange state of feeling well. Interweaving the chronicle of her cure with glimpses of the events and emotional turmoil that led her to embrace comforts of "being ill" even as a young girl, she recounts the difficulty and compromise that accompany her return to health, the grief she feels for the passing of the symptoms that once defined her and for the final silencing of the eight inner voices which had been her constant companions for as long as she could remember. She re-creates in vivid detail the terrors of "Prozac poop-out," when, without warning, the medication fails and symptoms of OCD return, and the small but vital victory she wrests during her frightening relapse with the emergence of "bits of self that manage to rise above the chemicals of illness, the chemicals of cure, and . . . for a moment take in the world."

Slater's first packet of Prozac works its wonders in only five days, less time than even her doctor, a staunch advocate of its powers, predicted. Liberated from the debilitating anxiety and pain that had circumscribed her life, Slater ventures into the world with the innocence and enthusiasm of a child. She wanders joyfully through Boston's Faneuil Hall, captivated by its irresistible array of foods, its extraordinary street performers, and the crowds of ordinary people pursuing ordinary pleasures. She allows herself the luxury of sleeping late for the first time in her life, attends her first rock concert, spends long, languid afternoons drinking lattes at outdoor cafés with newly acquired friends. Her body confirms the transformation: "I was the picture of health, as though I had finally come into the body meant for me." Armed with newfound confidence, she sends out her résumé ("to date, one of my finest pieces of fiction") and gets her first real job, as a teacher in a literacy center. After almost a year on Prozac, she is accepted at Harvard, where as a student in psychology she eventually earns a doctorate in record time. She falls in love with Bennett, a chemist who is willing to accept her simultaneous "love affair" with Prozac.

Like all love affairs, however, Slater's infatuation with the small green-and-cream pills demands sacrifices. There are practical repercussions: her creativity ebbs, her sex drive dwindles, and she learns that Prozac is an inconstant lover when she suddenly experiences a horrifying descent into "crazy," obsessive behavior. The emotional toll is at once more elusive and more profound. In the early months of her treatment, Slater is torn between her enthusiasm for the rewards and possibilities of health and a deep-seated fear of abandoning her "illness identity." "There was no more depression, which had felt like the stifling yet oddly comforting weight of a woolen blanket, or anxiety, which lent a certain fluorescence to things, or voices, which had always been there, sometimes louder, sometimes softer, some North Star of sound in the night." As time passes, she adjusts to Prozac's cool and calming effects and to the sporadic imperfections in its chemistry that allow odd bits of illness to break through. Now, after a decade on Prozac, she is resigned to her dependency on Eli Lilly and at the same time determined to exercise her freedom to reenvision the past and the present, to choose who she is and wants to be. "Prozac is not my lover any longer," she writes, "but over the long haul has become a close friend, a slightly anemic, well-meaning buddy whose presence can considerably ease pain but cannot erase it."

Today, Prozac has become the legal drug of choice of a whole generation, used by millions of people all over the world. It's been hailed as a wonder drug and condemned as a drug that triggers violence. While 40 to 50 percent of patients on Prozac experience sexual dysfunction, a group of Prozac-taking British women reported a rather more stimulating side effect: whenever they sneeze, they have orgasms. As one of the first people to take the drug and among the few who have stayed on it for ten years, and as a psychologist who has also been a psychiatric patient, Lauren Slater is in a unique position to shed light on both Prozac's immediate impact and its long-term effects. Her book supports neither the generally positive position found in Dr. Peter Kramer's widely acclaimed *Listening to Prozac* nor the backlash against it expressed in Peter Breggin's *Talking Back to Prozac*. Her territory lies outside and beyond the noisy controversy. With elegance and humor, she takes us directly inside the strange new world Prozac has created, and using the language and images of poetry, reveals its gifts and its burdens.

A Conversation with
Lauren Slater

Much has been written about Prozac, from both negative and positive points of view. What does Prozac Diary add to this ongoing dialogue?

To this dialogue *Prozac Diary* adds the voice of the consumer— myself—telling the story of pharmacological "cure" from an intimate, and, I hope, authentic stance. Writing about Prozac, as so many people have done, is really not at all the same as writing through Prozac, as I have done, and the portrait that emerges, although no more or less honest than the more distant, "objective" portraits, is a singular story with singular details that no amount of detached research could have uncovered.

In addition, *Prozac Diary* is meant to address directly the issues involved in long-term Prozac use, which are in many ways different from the issues and ethical dilemmas involved in relatively short-term Prozac use. I wrote my book with the partial intention of portraying what this drug is like when taken over a lifetime, the difficulties, the dangers, and the blessings; and my hope is that it will speak to other people considering, or already embarking on, long-term usage.

Your first book, Welcome to My Country, was primarily about patients you worked with, while Prozac Diary is a much more personal book. Which book did you find easier to write? How did the writing processes differ?

At some essential level, the writing process is always the same for me, no matter how different the project is. Writing, whether about myself or others, demands a rigorous imaginative stretch, a reach for lyricism that conveys emotion, as opposed to covering it. This is always my struggle.

That commonality aside, the two books did present different artistic problems. I think I found it easier to write about other people, about patients, because I could portray the enormity and dignity of their suffering without risking self-absorption, or blatant narcissism. In writing about myself, I feel much more constricted. I worry about solipsism, shortsightedness, self-aggrandizement, self-denigration, and all the other treacherous territories that come with the fascinating pursuit of autobiography.

You offer readers glimpses of your childhood in passages interspersed within the running narrative. Why did you choose this method, rather than presenting a straight chronology from the onset of your illnesses through your experiences with Prozac?

There is a fairly simple answer to this. I intended for *Prozac Diary* to be a book about cure, not illness. Thus, I self-consciously set out to avoid a linear illness narrative, a structure that would have placed as much weight on sickness as on health. Instead, I chose to give quick glimpses of the illness—enough, I hope, to convey its essential character, but not so much that it obscures my main purpose: to write about an emergence, not a descent.

In retrospect, what was the hardest part of crossing into "the land-scape of health"?

The hardest part for me was, and continues to be, my concern that I have lost some of the honesty and intensity that illness, which by its nature places one at the periphery of society, brought to my life. In Freud's famous essay "Mourning and Melancholia" he articulates this conflict extremely clearly. "The depressive has a keener eye for the truth than people who are not melancholic . . . we only wonder why a man has to be ill before he can come to truth of this kind."

Memories of your mother play a large role in your descriptions of your childhood. What was your relationship to your father like? How did your two sisters react to the atmosphere at home?

My relationship with my father was placid but fairly distant. His way of coping with the crises on the homefront was to absent himself, physically and emotionally. I don't remember him around a lot. As for my two sisters, they were treated quite differently than I. My mother adored my younger sister and treated my older sister with respect. However, they did not escape the trauma that comes from witnessing the cruelty she inflicted on myself and others. Their scars are different, but, I'm sure, deep.

One of the "side effects" of Prozac you experienced was a new interest in religion and spirituality. Did this help you adjust to the changes you were undergoing? Can you describe the spiritual aspects of mental illness— and of mental health?

My own belief is that spirituality, the idea, the feeling of a greater moral coherence to our world, is essential for people, in illness and in health. Health was a crisis for me, a new world, and I partially relied on my sense of spirituality to guide me through. This "sense" for me is rooted in moral conviction. We are, I believe, morally obligated to navigate the complexities of living with as much grace and courage as we can muster. So yes, my spiritual leanings certainly helped me adjust to the adventure that was, and is, Prozac.

As for the spiritual aspects of mental illness and health, that's a big question, one which would be answered differently by every person to whom the question was posed. For me, the spiritual aspects are the same whether in the sanguine or pathological state. Spirituality transcends illness and health. It is, for me, a fixed yet oddly fluid set of beliefs that serve as a guide. However, in illness I am less capable, in some ways, of responding to the moral challenge that spirituality is, while in health, I have more stamina and, perhaps, more courage. On the other hand, in health, in the pastel glow of good days, I often catch myself becoming slack, letting myself loose from the discipline that a spiritual life requires. Illness represents, in many senses, a reminder, a calling back to attend to all I've let slide.

In what ways have your own experiences as a psychiatric patient helped you as a psychologist?

I don't think my experiences as a psychiatric patient have been much help to me as a psychologist. I don't believe the suffering induced by mental illness necessarily makes a person more empathic to others. In fact, it may be just the opposite. Mental illness, for me, can be a painfully self-absorbed state that shuts out the world, and one's ability to connect to it.

Memoirs, particularly by women with dysfunctional or difficult family histories, have become quite popular today. Why do you think this is true? Did any of them influence your own memoir, and if so, in what way?

I have always been an autobiographical/biographical writer long before the "memoir" craze. I have had a powerful urge to document "real lives," as a means of directly communicating with other people. I love fiction, but it can feel like a veil to me, like a slanted way of saying something. Because, perhaps, I grew up in a home of lies and denial, I consistently crave art that is balder and somehow more stripped. So I actually don't think my own autobiographical writing was influenced by other memoirs, as I've been charting my life and the lives of others since I was a child. However, I do think the publication of my books, and any measure of publicity they have received, is probably entirely dependent on the popularity of the memoir in general.

As for the first part of the question, I don't know. I can hazard a few guesses. I can say for sure that I am fascinated by the phenomenal interest in the autobiographical form. Perhaps the public interest in this form has something to do with a collective sense that we are, as a culture, becoming increasingly less direct and honest, that we are ever more image-driven, that we know the media to distort and even lie, that we know our figureheads to distort and even lie. There is, perhaps, an ever-increasing sense that our world is warped, a place of funhouse mirrors and ever-shifting ground. In response, we want something solid, we want a real glimpse into real lives, and thus we grasp these books. That "these books" happen to contain much dysfunction in them is simply because any honest account, from Saint Augustine's *Confessions* to *The Liars' Club*, will, by necessity depict dysfunction. Real life is difficult, and difficulty leads to dysfunction. It's not the dysfunction we're after. It's the sense of truth, of authenticity.

What message does your book have for people who are not prescribed Prozac or other selective serotonin reuptake inhibitors?

I think, I hope, my book is about the search for and struggle with identity, about what constitutes a "real self," and these are questions that are pertinent to any sentient human being. In addition, there is no person in the developed world today who is not a part of the "Prozac Nation." SSRIs, and Prozac in particular, have influenced the brains and souls of everyone—those who swallow the pills, those who don't. We all know someone who is on Prozac, or think about going on it ourselves, or see it seep into our communities in ways both alarming and amusing. Prozac, for these reasons alone, is a remarkable drug. It is perhaps the only drug to have seeped so far out of its plastic shell, to have been absorbed by the bloodstreams of so very many, even those who have never had any tactile relationship with it. I would go so far as to say we are all "on" Prozac, in that we all must grapple with its presence, its meaning, and its implications for our lives.

Has your relationship with Prozac changed since writing the book?

My relationship with Prozac has changed somewhat since writing the book, although the change has nothing to do with the book's publication or creation. Since that time, however, I have had more trouble with the dreaded tolerance, and have had to increase my dose to levels so high they are over what the FDA recommends. Of course, this is frightening for many reasons—side effects, toxicity, permanent cognitive damage, no one really knows. I will wait and see what the future holds.

QUESTIONS FOR DISCUSSION

1.   For much of the book, Slater calls her doctor the "Prozac Doctor," rather than by name. How does this reflect her feelings about and her experience with the medical profession? Does the doctor's attitude justify this depersonalization, or does she expect too much of him? What does she mean when she says, "The Prozac Doctor was biblical to me"?

2.   Slater writes about her mother, "Nothing was ever enough, for there was no plug to stopper the hole in her soul, no pill." From the evidence in the book, do you think that Slater's mother had serious emotional problems? In what ways are Slater's symptoms a reaction against her mother's "manic intensity" and in what ways do they echo the very things she objects to about her mother? How much do Slater's own problems affect her descriptions of her mother, and how do they change in the course of the book?

3.   What purpose do the sections called "Letter to My Doctor" serve in the narrative? Why do you think Slater decided to juxtapose the cold clinical facts about her illness and her hauntingly poetic reminiscences about childhood?

4. Why did Slater wait four or five days before taking her first pill, despite the fact that she was clearly upset about her obsessive-compulsive disorder? Why did her dream about the Prozac Doctor make it possible for her to begin her medication?

5. Slater questions the assumption that health is "natural" and "good." Do you think the Judeo-Christian tradition and the medical profession accept this point of view too readily? Can illness offer insights that a "healthy" person might never discover?

6. Slater writes about the eight people she pictures living inside her: "three men who taunted me, three nine-year-olds, a girl trapped in a glass cage, and a blue baby, sometimes dead, sometimes dying." Based on what you know about Slater's life, what do you think these figures represent?

7. How did Slater's job at the literacy center help with her own healing process? In what ways is her passage from an illness identity to one of health similar to the transition her immigrant students are facing?

8. Slater compares Prozac to the drugs used in primitive cultures as a means of accessing the gods. Do you think this is a valid comparison? Does Prozac make Slater more spiritually aware or does it undermine her spirituality?

9. Why does Slater switch from a first-person narrative to a third-person narrative when she describes the actual events of her child-hood and the early signs of her illness?

10. How does Slater's diminished sexuality affect her sense of self? Is her ability to love more fully a fair "trade-off" for her lack of physical pleasure?

11.   Slater cites literature from Eli Lilly and other researchers that claim that the success of serotonin-specific chemicals like Prozac show that "the patient's past, the story of self, is no longer relevant. We do not need to explain mental illness in the context of history. We can place it, and its cures, firmly in the context of chemicals." Does Slater's own story support this conclusion?

12.   Some research suggests that Prozac actually improves one's personality rather than just eliminating symptoms of illness. Is it unethical or deceitful or even dangerous to use a drug in this way? Despite her acknowledgment that Prozac has changed her life, Slater reports that she feels both shame and guilt about her dependence on it. Do you sympathize with her feelings?

For information about other Penguin Readers Guides, please call the Penguin Marketing Department at (800) 778-6425, email at reading@penguinputnam.com, or write to us at:

Penguin Marketing Department CC
Readers Guides
375 Hudson Street
New York, NY 10014-3657

Please allow 4–6 weeks for delivery.
To access Penguin Readers Guides on-line, visit Club PPI on our Web site at: http://www.penguinputnam.com